Chosen for Riches

A LIFE-RELATED EXPOSITION OF EPHESIANS

Bob Hendren

Austin, Texas 78765

Dedication

To Joyce

with love
and appreciation for her support
while this book was being written.

A complete Teacher's Manual/Resource Kit
for use with this paperback is available
from your religious bookstore or the publisher.

All scripture quotations followed by the
superscript[1] are Hendren's
own translation from the Greek text.
Unless otherwise indicated,
scripture quotations are from the *Revised Standard
Version of the Bible,* copyrighted 1946, 1952, and
1971 by the Division of Christian Education, National
Council of Churches, and used by permission.

Library of Congress Catalog Card Number 77-25775
ISBN 0-8344-0096-0
5 4 3 2

Contents

Chosen 1

Time and distance have been virtually annihilated. In hours we cross distances that took our grandfathers weeks to travel. We talk instantly to someone at any point on the globe. Yet, interpersonal distances are still vast and deep. The generation gaps, sexual gaps, and social and international gaps are of such magnitude that mankind despairs of seeing them bridged.

The sickening feeling of being cut off from God is even greater than these profound gulfs.

Many people live with a vague ache and gnawing loneliness. Trained and educated to evaluate everything from a human point of view, these truly "lost" humans grope through life with little sense of purpose. They get involved in short-term relationships with no commitment to escape life's throbbing emptiness. They pursue sex, drugs, alchohol, stoicism, or ambition to ease the pain of lack of friendship with God or other human beings.

All these symptoms of separation from God are not new. An astounding similarity exists between our modern world and the world of the apostle Paul. Paul observed a pagan society that "had lost its nerve," filled with the despairing cynicism of people who could not find their way. Their concepts of both God and humanity, like ours, were distorted and hazy. People were used and manipulated by power-mad politicians and military rulers. "Bread and the games" was the cry of the once noble Roman plebian. Hatred, like a common virus, infected heart after heart.

It all sounds up-to-date. Like tomorrow's screaming headlines. The needs of such people were obvious to Paul. Just as ours would be. In touch as he was with God's grace, he could see that only a radical solution would work. No halfway measures! The haters and hated both needed a new perspective, the perspective of God. They needed to see themselves from God's viewpoint. Only a penetrating look at their sinful condition and the possibilities of grace could open up their hearts and clear their moral fogginess.

Paul presented God's plan for mankind with great clarity. It called for nothing less than to unite all men and women in a new humanity. A new relationship to God and one another through Jesus Christ was proposed and, in many cases, joyously accepted. Ephesians is Paul's presentation of God's great plan to get people to see things from His point of view. This epistle speaks eloquently to all ages, and even in our time of despair it holds forth the same shining hope of reconciliation and oneness.

The church in Ephesus was a microcosm of the world of its time, teeming with a mixture of paganism, mysticism, and violence. Acts 19 contains background information on Paul's ministry in Ephesus. Yet Paul's letter deals with more than the specific needs and problems of the Ephesians. In every sense, it is a sweeping resumé of God's great purpose in Christ and of the practical implications of accepting the lordship of Jesus.

Commentators often note these doctrinal and practical emphases, yet too much stress should not be placed on this division. Doctrine must never be separated from life. Salvation is not earned by mastering a quota of doctrine, but by allowing doctrine to shape our lives. Doctrine gives us right ideas about God and what God will make happen in our lives if we believe in Him.

God's Point of View (1:1-2)

Having right ideas about God is a central point in Ephesians. Paul says he is an apostle according to "the will of God." He approaches this letter and his whole ministry from God's viewpoint. The letter to the Ephesians is a look at the most important spiritual considerations from God's viewpoint.

Paul presents us God's tremendous challenge to look at Christ, look at spiritual blessings, look at the idea of the church, look at our salvation, look at our brother — look at everything from God's viewpoint! That is difficult because we usually evaluate everything by our own standards, making it hard for us to see things from another's point of view.

7

A true key to understanding another person is seeing things from his point of view. Indian sages said: "Say nothing evil of a man until you have walked eight days in his moccasins." Have you ever looked at an unflattering photo of yourself and said: "I don't like it, it's not me"? It's you from a viewpoint you don't care for.

We have a problem in seeing ourselves as God sees us. We may not like the picture! We must first be impressed with God before we can see things from his viewpoint and re-examine our life and mission.

Think of the encounter Isaiah had with God (Isa. 6). When Isaiah saw the Lord "high and lifted up" his whole perspective on himself and his mission changed. He recognized his sinfulness and dedicated his life to God's cause. Ephesians begins with the same objective. We confront the truly impressive actions of God and from our impression comes our loving response to God.

"Almost all wrong ideas about religion can be traced to wrong ideas about God."

Paul knows our problem: we are not sufficiently impressed with God and his action to save us. Man must know the God he is trying to respond to. That is why Paul pours out this great hymn of praise (1:3-14). This hymn (one sentence in the original) praises God the Father who plans and brings our salvation into action, God the Son who dies to redeem us, and God the Holy Spirit who dwells with us after our conversion. When we know what God has for us, we can respond in depth.

Almost all wrong ideas about religion can be traced back to wrong ideas about God. A materialistic, man-centered religion like the paganism of the Greeks can be traced to their inadequate views on God. Present-day believers who stress unthinking duty and a lockstep mentality reflect their inadequate view of God. They view him as some sort of universal bully who passes out senseless orders to obey! After all, he is in charge.

Paul, however, presents a balanced and incisive view of God in action. He wants us to understand and appreciate the love, planning, and direction that has passed from God to man. We will call God blessed when we see our salvation and enjoyment of his spiritual blessings.

Chosen in Love (1:3-4)

We are chosen! The top line on our list of spiritual blessings is our selection by God as objects of his love and mercy (1:4). We have been "picked out" as a man rescues a valuable object from a garbage can. God chose his people before the foundation of the world. This is not a theological riddle; it is a tribute to God's graciousness.

God wants us to have limitless treasures in Christ. He also has a great goal for us — that we should be "holy and blameless before him." He chose us to represent his own glory and grace to a decadent world. It is a gracious choice, reminding us of God's words to Israel (Deut. 7:6-8):

9

For you are a people holy to the Lord your God; the Lord your God has chosen you to be a people for his own possession, out of all the peoples that are on the face of the earth. It was not because you were more in number than any other people that the Lord set his love upon you and chose you . . . but it is because the Lord loves you . . . .

Three conceptions emerge from God's choice. First, any sharing in God and his blessings is only to be on the basis of his choice. No one is going to invite himself into fellowship with God, but he enters that relationship on God's terms.

Second, God's community of believers is no accident of history. God's people come into a relationship with him and with one another solely as the result of deliberate and well-planned action by God. It was no novel idea or last-minute decision.

Third, God knows our nature and needs even before we do. He stood ready to help us "before the foundation of the world." What a contrast exists between God's readiness to help and our unawareness.

When our first baby came into toddler-hood, my wife and I were quite unprepared for the collection of skinned knees and scrapes an active toddler accumulates. I found myself making hasty trips to get bandages and antiseptic. Soon we learned to have it on hand — "just in case." Of course, the fact that bandages were in the medicine cabinet did not force her to skin her knees. We were ready, though, in case she did. We had finally learned her nature.

God also knows our nature. He was prepared in advance to meet our needs. That is the sure mark of a loving Father who truly cares.

Chosen First

You must not be worthless because you've been chosen by the best!

All of us have been rejected in this life, perhaps by friends, by parents at times, by our associates, or on some other level, personal or impersonal. We've been cut from the team, turned down for a job, or rejected by a loved one.

During World War II, anyone who was classified as a reject for military service was designated "4-F" by the draft board. Songs were written about those miserable 4-Fs. Girls would not date 4-Fs. They were mocked and ridiculed. At times all of us have been 4-F. These rejections hurt, and they confirm our mistaken opinion that we are worthless.

Still, Paul says, God has chosen us. He does not just tolerate us, or half-heartedly permit us to hang around the edge of his group. He has chosen us for "every spiritual blessing . . . in Christ" (1:3)[1].

I remember vividly being a boy in elementary school in Memphis. My slender little body (they called it skinny back then) was not attractive to those mighty muscular athletes who chose the daily sports teams. As teams were chosen, I shrunk back in dread with the other cast-offs. We knew what was coming. First, all the smug, superior athletic types were selected. You could tell they were acutely aware of their muscular virtues and expected a first or, at worst, a second place pick. Somewhere along after

11

the stronger girls, I was reluctantly selected. Naturally, I ended up with some exalted position such as one of two or three right fielders. Hardly in the history of that school did anyone ever hit a ball to right field. I also played back-up catcher and kept the ball from going into the street!

Occasionally, a friend would get to choose teams, and a wonderful thing would happen. There were days when I was chosen right up there with the elite, and even got to pitch.

"Through no merit or ability of my own, I was chosen, but solely because a friend did the choosing."

So it is with God's choice. We have no ability, no claim on his grace, no spiritual muscles to flex in his face. We have nothing but our need of a friend. Our Friend chooses us. Who could say no to being on such a team?

God's choice, moreover, is not an aimless one. It has a purpose. God does not call us to the "hot pursuit of unexamined goals," as one contemporary writer remarked, but he wants us to be "holy and blameless before him in love" (1:4).[1] So many aimless choices are scattered throughout our lives. Even a serious choice like a life partner is often made with emphasis upon nothing more than attractiveness or material security.

How can there be any growth from such aimless choices? The idea of being "holy and blameless" gives content and direction to God's choice. Being holy (the same root idea is in the word "saint") means "being dedicated and consecrated to God and useful for his purposes." A saint is not some smug and superior spiritual entity. He is challenged to become more like the holy God who has not chosen him randomly. We have been chosen so that we may be God's people, useful to him. We have not only been chosen, we have been allowed to pitch!

Adopted as Sons (1:5)

We are not invited merely to the outer limits of fellowship with God, we are "adopted as sons" into his family. We are not stranded on the outskirts of the kingdom. An adopted child is chosen deliberately to enjoy all privileges of access and love the parent may provide. A little adopted girl was chided by one of the natural children about her adoption. She replied, "Daddy and Mother *had* to take you, but they picked me out of the whole world."

All our brothers and sisters in the church share this family relationship. This idea of the church as a family is one of the most instructive in scripture. We "are all sons of God, through faith." Paul reminds us in Galatians 3:26-27 "for as many as were baptized into Christ have put on Christ." Later he tells us we are no longer slaves, but sons (Gal. 4:7).

What incalculable harm has been done in the church by those with a slave mentality rather than a son mentality! We must realize that those in the church are not fellow-members of some spiritual chain gang. They are members of our spiritual family and together we are objects of our Father's love and

13

concern. We love them and share a common affection because we have a common Father. We are in the same family.

When my family meets, I want to be with them. When we sit down at the supper table together, it is not because someone has ordered us to do it. We love to be together — it's a great privilege.

I also treasure communication with my personal family. When I was in the Marine Corps before marriage, I could hardly wait for mail call to see if I had received a letter from Joyce, my wife-to-be. When a letter came, nobody had to order me to read it. I read it upside down, sideways, between the lines. I even smelled it! I never saw anyone at mail call throw a letter away, or lay it aside unopened and say: "It's just a letter from my girl friend, I'll read it after I go have a Coke." None of that — instead they devoured letters like starving men eat food!

Isn't it strange that members of God's family have to be hounded to read letters from our heavenly Father? What a joy it should be to read good news from our Father telling us of his love and giving us direction for our lives. We're in the family of God. No one has to order us to come home at night to our family. When our family in God meets, we want to be there with them and with our heavenly Father. We're in the family — it makes a big difference in our spiritual life when we claim that blessing.

His Glorious Grace (1:6)

All through this section of Ephesians we hear Paul's glorious refrain: "To the praise of his glorious grace." The apostle never tired of God's grace. He stressed it always, everywhere, constantly. In his great treatises on grace, Romans and Galatians, he demonstrates that to abandon the grace concept is to abandon God. We cannot say, "Your emphasis is grace and mine is human endeavor" (Gal. 1:6).

Human pride hates grace. Human pride wants man to believe that he can pull himself up by his own spiritual bootstraps. But salvation by human achievement is impossible.

Only a divine solution could bring deliverance from our wretched slavery in sin. We must be as impressed with God's grace as Paul was. We cannot skip by it with a neat little definition and spend all of our time discussing the human response to grace. Our response is vital to receive God's grace, but the response does not earn grace. Our response must come from a heart deeply aware that salvation originates in God's love.

Grace testified to the incredible lengths God was willing to go to secure our redemption from sin. Grace cost God his son.

Redeemed by Blood (1:7-10)

Redemption means a price has been paid for our liberation from sin. We may have enough money to buy every cow in Texas, make a ski resort out of Mt. Everest, or hire the Green Bay Packers as our personal bodyguards. But we do not have enough money to secure personal freedom from sin, even one sin.

Our misdeeds are forgiveable only at the cost of the blood of the Son of God. There is no magic wand to wave, no arbitrary public address announcement from heaven of divine amnesty. Only God's solution provided in God's way — the way of the cross — can bring redemption. Grace has made the impossible possible — I can be forgiven, I am forgiven, I will be forgiven.

God has made known to us the mystery of his will (1:9). No one forced God to do this. He gave it freely and generously as a token of good pleasure. The word "mystery" means an open secret, open to the one who desires to know what God wills, but closed to the one who avoids God. As the mathematician Pascal said: "There is light enough for him to see who chooses to, and darkness enough for him who chooses not to."

This open secret, at one time concealed, but now available, tells of God's daring arrangement enacted at just the right opportunity (1:10). This arrangement or "dispensation" (the word in the original means a plan, administration, or arrangement) of God is to "unite (sum up) all things in Christ." God proposes to make Christ the center and unifier of everything.

The verbal infinitive "to unite all things" comes from a Greek verb which is rare in ancient literature. It means "to bring something to a head" or "to put various parts together in such a way that they are now whole."

The idea of "summary" seems to be that Christ is designated by God as the only One in whom any kind of real togetherness can be found. Christ is the one designed by God to put it all together. He is the only one who is big enough to hold our world or ourselves together (see Col. 1:16-17). Only in him can there be effective unity. Christ puts us together in a truly new way (1:10). We are not bits of debris in the population explosion, but parts of a new humanity put together in a fresh way by Christ.

Our Spiritual Inheritance (1:11-14)

Paul's use of the pronouns "we" and "us" means God's chosen people were a part of old and new Israel. No one will be excluded from the new Israel because of his role. Paul shifts to his Gentile subjects by using "you" and adds the important word "also," indicating the Gentiles also share in the Spirit which "guarantees" their inheritance as well (1:13-14)! Therefore, all the blessings of God's inheritance are available to all people who will put their trust in Christ.

Our inheritance is a spiritual blessing, not a material property transaction. God gives his inheritance, not to those who possess certain physical property, but to those adopted by grace into his family. The idea of a guarantee is "a lasting right to this blessing," part of the Old Testament idea of the word (1:14).

Rich insights into the word "guarantee" (*arrhabon* in Greek) have been provided by discoveries made in ancient papyri documents. The basic sense of the word in business transactions of that time is of a *part* given in advance of what would be *fully* given at a later time. For example, one ancient document tells of a certain Lampon, a mouse-catcher, who was paid eight *drachmae* as an advance (*arrhabon*) "that he may catch the mice while they are with young."

17

In the first century the word "guarantee" also was used in another form to mean "a betrothed bride." Another culture used the word to mean "an engagement ring." Thus Paul wants us to know that God *guarantees* his inheritance to those who have expressed their trust in Christ by giving them the Holy Spirit as He promised (Acts 2:38,39; 5:32).

The Holy Spirit in our lives is God's assurance that, while being a Christian now is great, even more wonderful things are ahead. God has given us a "pledge" on this. Now a pledge or guarantee must be actually possessed, as you must hold onto your warranty or guarantee for it to be effective. You must remain a believer living by faith. The possession of the Spirit himself is a dimension of that faith.

The Spirit was not given so that we might have better and more vivid experiences than others. Rather, the Spirit is a dramatic reminder that our God has especially chosen us and shares himself with us now. He also will see us through completely to our full inheritance. He has done everything to make our ultimate salvation possible. We are to be his — to the praise of his glorious grace!

Prayer 2

The doctrine of God presented here by Paul shows that all believers share in the riches of Christ. Doctrine gives us right ideas about God, but the ideas must be applied. Paul uses a prayer to further enlighten his readers. He wants them to get the big picture and open their hearts to all God is trying to do with them.

Paul knew he could pray effectively for the Ephesian Christians to grow spiritually because they had the right foundation. They had faith and love (1:15). Great lives are built on "faith in the Lord Jesus and love toward all the saints." Their faith was in the right object—Jesus—and their love was non-discriminatory—"for all the saints."

Paul looked for something to build upon. He wanted to supply what was needed to assist in spiritual growth. Paul did not believe it was his responsibility to look for all the negative aspects in the lives of others. He looked for what could be built upon, knowing that good growth has the power to displace the bad.

Paul's Prayer and Ours (1:16)

Paul knew the faith of the Ephesians was not abstract. It was based upon reality, and Paul prayed for what could grow out of their faith and love. Prayer in the Bible is not wishful thinking. Prayer is not an emergency flare shot up from the shores of spiritual apathy. Prayer is a discipline that gets us even deeper into the positive will of God for all our lives (1 John 5:14).

Yet, often we miss the point of prayer. We may think of prayer as a "duty." We think, "It is our *duty* to pray for so and so . . .," then we crank out a few pious phrases and lapse into nonproductive silence.

We often wait until we are bone-weary, usually at bedtime, and launch a barrage of spiritual generalizations toward God: "Lord, bless all the sick in the whole world," or "God, help the world to be a better place to live in . . . ." We interrupt our prayers with little episodes of mind-wandering, then apologetically return and address God: "Now where was I?" A performance like this might remind God of some rerun movie on TV which is constantly interrupted with a never-ending series of pointless commercials.

It is also not unusual for us to drift off to sleep in the middle of "prayer" and leave God waiting on the other end until morning. Imagine a person rude enough to drift off to sleep in the middle of a long-distance call to his best friend. Yet this is the way we treat our God at times!

20

It is no accident that Paul's discussion moves from God's great gifts to prayer. God's people have always been praying people. But today an arid desert of noncommitment surrounds the believer, and prayer to some seems outmoded. A bumper sticker reads, "Honk if you believe anything."

Christians are easily affected by this atmosphere. Is an intense prayer life becoming rare among Christians? Henry Higgins, the elocutionist in *My Fair Lady*, said, "The Americans haven't spoken English in years." Could it be said of many of us: "They haven't prayed meaningfully in years"?

Our problem may be that we look at prayer as one more spiritual duty. Why does God want us to pray? Just another case of submitting an unnecessary report — so much busy work? No! Prayer is to be productive communication as it was with Jesus.

A Way of Life

Prayer was a way of life with Jesus. His prayer life was so intense it caused his disciples to ask: "Teach us to pray . . ." (Luke 11:1). Jesus' reply has been called the "Lord's Prayer" (though it has been perceptively recognized by some as being truly the disciples' prayer).

In this prayer Jesus wants us to recognize the greatness and generosity of the personal God. He is "our Father," not some magical force or "first cause uncaused." Jesus asks us to place God's priorities ahead of everything else. God's kingdom (his reign in the hearts of men) has priority over human needs.

21

Jesus recognizes a place for our needs, however. They are not belittled. They are important and have a place in prayer "every day." A person is not more holy if he is hungry. Material needs are not to be omitted from prayers to make them more spiritual. Spiritual needs such as forgiveness for sins and power over temptations must also receive adequate consideration.

Jesus' insight into prayer reveals that he outlined a productive approach to praying. Jesus' approach emphasizes our relationship to God as Father. Jesus says, "Pray this way: 'Our Father. . . .'"[1] Prayer is the communication which allows this father-child relationship to grow. No relationship develops without communication. A constant problem in families is the lack of real communication. The relationship cannot expand unless the communication expands.

"Our 'amens' should be commas, not periods, in our prayer life with God."

Paul reveals this communicative aspect of prayer to the Ephesians by affirming his unceasing prayer on their behalf (1:16). Prayer, like good communication, is not finished at some predictable point. Our "amens" should be commas, not periods, in our prayer life with God. A man was once chided by his wife because he never told her he loved her anymore. "Well," he said defensively, "I told you once. If I ever change my mind I'll let you know."

Relationships don't work that way. Like Paul, we must pray "without ceasing" (1 Thess. 5:17, KJV).

Christianity is a relationship between a dependent, needy human being and his heavenly Father. Prayer helps that relationship deepen.

Content is also important in communication. It does not always have to be profound, but it must be honest. A husband and wife who share the little details of their lives are building a marriage which will survive the big and devastating emergencies. Our prayer life with God must deal with both the humdrum and the heavenly.

Praying with Purpose (1:17-23)

Paul uses a prayer to relate the contents of prayer (1:17-23). It is a specific prayer with direct objectives, calling upon God to change the lives of receptive Christians. The fact that a Christian's life is *already changed* means he can pray. By praying he reinforces the direction of the change as "unto Christ."

Paul never lacks objectives for prayer. He has obviously spent a great deal of time praying and analyzing the deepest prayer needs of his brethren. Indeed, much of the inner heart of the letters he wrote can be seen in the prayer objectives. This is certainly true in Ephesians as Paul reveals his spiritual maturity in knowing where the Ephesian Christians are and where they need to be. What could be better than praying for God to accomplish just those specific objectives?

Paul prays — "the God of our Lord Jesus Christ, the Father of glory, may give you a spirit of wisdom and of revelation in the knowledge of him, having the eyes of your hearts enlightened, that you may know what the hope of your calling is, what the riches of his glorious inheritance is among the holy ones, and what the surpassing greatness of his power is toward us who believe, a power that is energized by his powerful might and effected in his resurrection of Christ from the realm of the dead" (1:17-23).[1]

Paul prays for God to give them wisdom (1:17). Strength without wisdom is nothing. The strength of their foundation of love and faith will depend on the continued exercise of wisdom. Isocrates, the Athenian orator of the fourth century B.C., recognized this connection:

> . . . If all the athletes should acquire twice the strength they now possess, the rest of the world would be no better off; but let a single man attain to wisdom, and all men will reap the benefit who are willing to share his insight.
> —Panegyricus 1

Wisdom guarantees continued faith and love.

Our eyes need to be opened to the death-conquering might of God. He invaded time and history and rendered death powerless and ineffective. Christ's experience is to become our experience, for Christ's actions are the ground of our faith, the surety of our hope, and the motive to our labor of love.

We cannot generate any experience to surpass Christ's experiences. God calls us to share in Christ's actions on our behalf. We are converted to

Christ through sharing by faith in the redemptive acts of Christ. In our faith encounter with Christ in the act of baptism, for instance, we discover that it means identification with Christ's death, burial, and resurrection (Rom. 6:1-4).

In our lives as Christians we discover that continued contact with Christ provides renewed strength and victory in daily living. John underscores this point in his first epistle. The Christian must realize that he is not sinless, but in recognizing his sin and confessing it he finds that the experience of Christ's death (His blood) cleanses him from his sins (1 John 1:5-10).

We draw strength from Christ's experiences. They are real acts in history, testified to by competent witnesses. At best, our own experiences are pale images. Therefore, we take the experiences of Christ as our surety. They have been demonstrated to work!

Called to Hope (1:18)

The call of God is a call of hope (1:18). Like prayer, hope in the Bible never means wishful thinking, but confident expectation of reward. We are confident because our hope is in God, not ourselves. Our calling inspires a real hope because it is God who has called us through the gospel of his Son. God's invitation is serious business. He does not send out frivolous summons. As someone said, "If you *can know* you're saved five minutes after your baptism, why not five years later?" You can, if you have confidence in God and you remain firm in that conviction.

25

God did not send his Son to create a group of uncertain, anxious disciples. Jesus inspires us with a hope real enough and strong enough to bring life to people living in despair.

The same power that activated or energized the resurrection is behind our hope. Paul uses that very word—*energeo*—in verse 19.

What is this energy, or power? Power connects us with limitless spiritual resources. The resources of God! Why did Jesus pray in the Garden of Gethsemane? To evade his responsibility? No. Prayer was the connection by which God's power confirmed him in his purpose and strengthened him for the dark hours ahead (Mark 14:32-42).

Immeasurable Power

Think of the days before World War II when Winston Churchill looked on the growing menace of Nazi Germany with dismay. He had full insight into the dangers ahead. He knew what steps should be taken. Yet, he was powerless to act in any official capacity. He could do nothing except raise his voice and look on with anguish. But when the King asked him to become Prime Minister, then the resources of the empire were available. He had to act within the law of the land, but at last he could do something about the difficulties that faced the nation. He had access to strength far greater than that of one man alone.

Paul says that God's immeasurable power is "in us who believe" (1:19). God's power is in us. He does not provide his power to satisfy our whims, but to work in our weakness and remedy our lack of strength (2 Cor. 12:8-10). The thorn in the flesh remains, but God's power buoys up the apostle so that grace sustains him in his weakness.

God's power comes to us in our temptations to provide a way out (1 Cor. 10:13). God's power comes to us in our timidity to affirm that his Spirit strengthens us to be strong, sound, and self-controlled (2 Tim. 1:7). God's power raises us to deathless eternity (1 Cor. 15:43-44) when the "last enemy" destroys our earthly body.

We are also called to share in a bountiful treasury of *riches* in Christ (1:18). Our inheritance is a glorious one and we do not deserve it. Christians find an immense reward: being included in God's gracious will as heirs to the most glorious inheritance of all — eternal life! When the Bible says we are "heirs," it means we are *legitimate* sons of God.

Sometimes questions of God's rewards bother people. They shrink away from the idea of a rich reward in Christ because they believe it is too mercenary. While a few uninformed persons may look upon Christianity as a brand of "fire insurance," I believe C.S. Lewis was right when he said, "There is nothing in heaven that a mercenary soul could desire." Enjoying Christ is the treasure!

A lover of classical music could not be called mercenary if he wanted to attend an all–Mozart concert. A man in love with his wife would not be a mercenary if he wanted to spend his days with her. A Christian is no mercenary when he claims the hope of eternity with his Savior. No greater reward for the true Christian exists, for he knows that beyond the gifts there is the Giver!

The Power of Prayer (1:19)

Then, there is power (1:19). Power is one of our greatest needs. What good are the multitude of gadgets we have without power to run them? What use are our powerful automobiles without gasoline to keep them moving? On a recent outing, a group of young men all hit the showers at about the same time one morning. They lined up in the bathroom to dry their hair with portable dryers. They all plugged in at the same time and the inevitable happened. A fuse blew. What good were the dryers then? All they could do was wave the dryers like funeral-parlor fans! There was no power.

The church is the same way. Members of Christ's body must have the power of God in Christ available in our daily lives. Our own power is totally insufficient. At best, we are like little flashlight batteries trying to power a huge searchlight when we try to live without God's power. God does not want battery-powered Christians, but believers who are in constant contact with the real power source. After all, batteries soon corrode and start leaking acid.

In retrospect, we can see Paul is praying for the Ephesians to realize they have access to unlimited power in their present lives. God demonstrated his power in Jesus' resurrection. We know this power is available now for "the believers" (1:19)[1] because the participle translated "believers" is present. Great power is available to people "continuously practicing a life of believing in Christ."

How can I raise my standard of belief to this level? The great impression about God, which Paul creates in 1:3-14, gives insight into power that can lift the level of faith. Michael Collins, an astronaut, said after returning from space flight: "My threshold for measuring what is important has been raised." Paul's prayer was based on a high view of God, and ours must be also. If we see God as the giant at the top of the spiritual beanstalk or as an eye in the sky, no wonder we have problems. We must have a biblical concept of God before we can have a biblical concept of prayer and power.

Then there is the future aspect. We can experience a glorious inheritance. We can know the inheritance is real because our knowledge is based, not on our feeble and limited response, but on the dynamic action of God to whom we have responded.

The Body of Christ (1:20-21)

Paul develops the idea of the church as the body of Christ more fully in Ephesians 4. Here he introduces the tremendous concept of the exalted Christ. Even in his exaltation, he is the Christ of the church. He is not separate from his body, the church. To be in the church is to share in the exaltation of Christ, his victory over death, and all other spiritual powers. To be connected to Christ is to be in a dynamic spiritual relationship with the Ruler of all things and all entities. Prayer is vital to nurture that relationship.

Narrow ideas of the church do not come from God. He gave the church the greatest universal setting and purpose. Men have narrowed and diminished the idea of the church. We need a fresh insight into God's great plans for this community of believers in Christ.

Jesus Seen Today (1:22-23)

To begin to understand the greatness of the church, we must begin to understand the greatness of Christ. The church is his idea (Matt. 16:13ff), not ours. It is his body, not ours. The church is the group over which he is the head. Men must allow the church to remain Christ's property, his people, his organism. We need to notice the implications of verse 23. The church is "his body, the fullness of Him who is filling all things in all ways."[1] Actually the language leaves us with more than one possibility, but a suggestion by C.F.D. Moule is likely to be the correct one. The church is to be the completion of Christ who will, as the church grows unto him, be totally completed. The church demonstrates the reality of Christ's presence in the world as his body comes closer and closer to developing his character.

Paul says Christians are to be "conformed to the image of God's Son" (Rom. 8:29).[1] The essential mission of the church is to represent the life of Christ in the world. What is the overriding work of the church? To let the fullness of Christ be seen!

The opening thoughts of Ephesians focus on the great riches God shares with us. He has provided so much for us to build our lives upon. Because of God's great actions to bless us in Christ, we can grow as Christians. Fundamental to this growth is a strong prayer relationship with our Father. God is working through the church to show the fulness of Christ to the world. For each of us this means God has given us life — life apart from the deadly effects of sin.

Riches 3

In typing I am often made aware of the blessings of the electric typewriter. With it I can make mistakes twice as fast as with a manual. Modern technology does not keep us from making errors. In fact, sometimes it compounds them. So with all our technology and science, we are still sinners in need of God's grace. The scientific thinkers who brought us miracle drugs had compatriots who brought us destructive atomic weapons. Even at his greatest, man is a creature "dead in his trespasses and sins."

Sinful man is still the center of his own universe, imprisoned in the deceitful web of his own misdeeds. His education has not delivered him. In many cases, it has compounded his problem.

People often try to reject the biblical description of man as a sinner. They ignore Isaiah's statement (Isa. 59:2): "Your iniquities have made a separation between you and your God, and your sins have hid his face from you . . . ." "The sin theory," they say, "is degrading to man. It gives him complexes and inhibitions."

Even psychological theorists of recent times supported the biblical description of sin. The writings of such men as O.H. Mowrer, William Glasser, and Karl Menninger reveal the resurgence of a moral point of view in psychology. Mowrer, for example, in his startling work *The Crisis in Psychiatry and Religion,* states:

> For several decades we psychologists looked upon the whole matter of sin and moral accountability as a great incubus and acclaimed our liberation from it as epoch-making. But at length we have discovered that to be 'free' in this sense, i.e. to have the excuse of being 'sick' rather than *sinful,* is to court the danger of also becoming lost (p. 52).

Of course, the psychological pendulum may swing back again. You cannot base your life on what school of psychology is in vogue. Yet these men have sensed the biblical truth about what has happened to mankind.

Worth Redeeming

Instead of degrading man, however, biblical accounts tell of man's worth. How can this be? All other positions label man as a helpless creature "beyond freedom and dignity." Man, according to these views, is utterly incapable of resisting tendencies to wrong himself or others. He is a mere worm of a being who "oozed up out of the ooze" and cannot be held accountable.

Paul knows better. He sees men as fallen persons who need to rise to God's call for cleansing and renewal, life and true freedom. Man can be great, not by denying his sin, but by relying on God to deal with it. God restores man to personal freedom and dignity. Only in God is true humanity possible.

Jesus said the prodigal son "came to himself" before he returned to his father. To come to ourselves is to desire a restoration of broken fellowship with our Father. To accept a lesser appreciation of ourselves is to sell ourselves at the Devil's close-out sale for rejects.

God believes we are worth redeeming. Satan tries to convince us we are valueless. We know we are worth something to God, rather we are worth Someone. It cost God his Son to make us what we ought to be.

Shouting at Dead Men (2:1)

We are dead in our trespasses and sins (2:1). We were not merely sick, we were dead. A dead man possesses no capabilities. He is beyond *human* help. It's pointless to shout at a dead man: "All right there you, you're in bad shape I know, but pull yourself together and get up!" Such wasted words.

No psychological techniques, no positive thinking, no do-it-yourself schemes will help. No rescue is at hand without divine help. Only God's power in Jesus can raise us from the grave of sin.

We must be spiritually and morally raised from the dead. In this condition we do not go to God suggesting several options. We must agree to his direction and conform ourselves to his demands on

33

us. We demand nothing, but by grace receive everything.

Children of Wrath (2:2-3)

We are accountable for our sin, Paul says, even though we were influenced by the evil ruler of disobedient mankind (2:2). We submitted to the will of the lust of the flesh and of the mind (2:3). Had we taken less time rationalizing and excusing our behavior, we would have become aware of our transgressions.

The consequences of our sin are more vast than we could ever imagine. We deserve only God's wrath. Paul here is not developing the ideas of Romans 5 concerning human involvement in the consequences of the Adamic rebellion. Instead, he points to the consequences of being "dead in trespasses and sins." The natural result of this would be for God's wrath to deservedly come upon us. It is to be expected that we would inherit only wrath for our actions. But *instead* God's love brought grace to us in Jesus Christ.

Notice that Paul affirms that both Jews and Gentiles deserve "wrath." Wrath is not God's petulance. He does not hold a grudge against mankind. Instead, wrath here means God is set against sin, and cannot and will not condone it. But he can and will forgive the penitent sinner who responds in faith.

Heavenly Life Now (2:4-7)

Some statements in the Bible are great sources of profound meaning. The "I am" statements of John's

34

gospel are good illustrations. Jesus says, "I am the bread of life." What a world of meaning is compressed into that statement! Jesus claims to be sustainer, source, the very heart, and staff of life itself. "By grace are you saved through faith" (2:8)[1] is such a statement, but the introductory passage before it is pivotal in order to understand it.

We deserve only God's wrath (2:3). But God is "rich in mercy" and "loved us with a great love (2:4)."[1] Therefore, we can be delivered from what we actually deserve. The dead can be raised in Christ, so that Christ's resurrection is shared with us (2:5, 2 Cor. 4:7-14).

God also causes us to share in Christ's exaltation. We have been "caused to sit down together with Christ in the heavenly spheres (2:6)."[1] We share in a heavenly life now. We have in Christ a taste of the exaltation of heaven. This is why salvation by grace is so joyous and fulfilling — it introduces us to abundant living.

To be seated with God is to be sharing in God's reign. It means that the heavenly order of things is a present reality in our lives. We are already citizens of heaven (Phil. 3:20).

We are "aliens" to the world order (1 Pet. 2:11). But even though we are not of this world, we have a mission to this world. We must share the heavenly viewpoint with others and help them see beyond despair and defeat, so they too can begin their heavenly walk now. In a real sense, we "die and go to heaven" when we die to self in our conversion to Christ (Rom. 6:1ff).

35

"By grace are you saved" (2:5).[1] The verb "saved" in the perfect tense is a participle. An expanded translation would read: "by grace you are in a saved condition." You are now saved and exist in that state by the grace of God. Your share of the heavenly life (2:6) is a triumphant demonstration of God's grace. No person is beyond God's reach.

Answering God's Grace (2:8)

Verse eight is a bit different from verse five. The word "grace" in verse five does not have a definite article, so it is highly descriptive of the nature of God's saving of lost humans. It was a "grace" response on God's part to save us. In verse eight, however, Paul adds the definite article. Here the idea is to focus attention on the grace described above as being specifically available by faith: "This grace, this very grace I mentioned above, is actually possible for those of us who believe!"[1]

The whole action of God toward us in Christ is a gracious outreach. Heavenly life is "by grace," and it is only possible to share in it "through faith." Faith and grace are companions. Faith on man's part is the only appropriate answer to God's grace.

Faith in the Bible suggests "a readiness to respond to God and receive from God." Our faith adds *nothing* to the cross. Jesus alone did that. Our faith does, however, receive and respond to what the cross provides for us.

"This is not of yourselves, it is God's gift" (2:8).[1] What gift does the word "this" refer to? Grace, faith, or salvation? Actually the word "this" is, in the original, a neuter pronoun. Faith and grace are feminine nouns, and the word "salvation" is a participle (masculine). Neuter pronouns usually serve as references to the whole concept or idea in a passage. So "this" suggests that grace, faith, and salvation are all gifts of God.

"We could have no faith unless Christ had come to die for us, and that was God's act."

We can easily accept "grace" and "salvation" as gifts, but isn't "faith" a human response? How could it be a gift of God? Paul does not mean that faith comes as an overwhelming force from without. Why then would believers have any moral responsibility to turn from their sins and seek God? "Couldn't they just wait around for God to act?" "Well," Paul would say, "God has already acted in Christ, so get busy and accept God's great gift."

Rather than stressing the human response, Paul praises God's initiative in making faith possible. Paul says that everything about Christianity has its ultimate source in God. We could have no faith unless Christ had come to die for us, and that was God's act.

By sending Christ, God is ultimately responsible for our faith possibilities. If God had not sent Christ, in what would we have faith? If we had not heard the gospel telling us of God's gracious calling, to what would we have responded? We cannot be saved by faith in faith, but by faith in Christ. We truly bring

37

nothing to God except our need! Our response is necessary, yet God has graciously made that response possible.

The Appreciative Response

God has given us the object for our faith, his Son. Our response is called "faith" in this passage. Since this is such a comprehensive summary passage of our salvation, we must assume that the terms are used with their widest possible meaning. We know that "grace" adequately covers all that God has done and will continue to do for man. "Faith" then must express the total human response to grace. God's gift of his Son calls for a response on our part that is both appreciative and appropriate.

The nature of an event or action determines the appropriate response. A Marine Corps drill instructor who is yelling at a recruit to stand at attention does not expect the recruit to give him an essay on the values of relaxation. He expects the recruit to "snap to" instantly. The recruit who fails to learn the appropriate response is in trouble.

Our response to God, however, is not like that. The recruit's response is appropriate, but not very appreciative. The nature of the cross is such that the more we appreciate it, the more appropriate is our response. When we realize how magnificent God's grace is, we will see that the only right response is to have faith in God. We do not have faith in Christ merely because God has "ordered" us to. We have faith because it is the appropriate and appreciative response to grace.

We must realize that without God's action there would be no salvation. This sort of gratitude would eliminate any element of human "dickering" about the conditions of salvation. A man dying of hunger appreciates the good food that is offered him. He does not quibble about the plate it is served on. We cannot create our own conditions of salvation.

The Appropriate Response

Our response must also be appropriate. We would laugh at anyone who said: "What a cute sunset that is tonight!" A response like that is inappropriate.

We can not respond appropriately to God without his word, so we must listen to his directions. God's laws and directions tell us the way things are spiritually. Some laws are arbitrary. For example, is there any intrinsic reason why red should mean stop? If people agreed on it, couldn't lavender or orange mean stop?

There are other "laws," however, which are not like this. The law of gravity, for example. We cannot repeal this law no matter how much we may desire. An appropriate response is always necessary, regardless of the law's source.

Similarly, we must learn that the spiritual universe, to use a metaphor, is not a world of arbitrary and nonsensical notions under the general heading of "God says." Rather, God reveals the way things *really are* spiritually. Christ really had to die; there was no other way. He knew this in the garden. He knew there were no other options. The situation was one that called for only one possible response — the cross.

39

There are no options in the spiritual universe, no arbitrary decisions. God reveals what *is*. We are sinners. Christ had to die for us. We must avail ourselves of God's grace. There is no other way. We are either saved by grace through faith, or we are not saved at all. Nothing but faith on our part is an appropriate response.

A Total Response

This comprehensive response of faith is appropriate because it answers the saving action of God's grace. When we seriously consider our alienation from God was as a total being (in body, in emotions, and in mentality) we see the need for a total response. Our sin has alienated us from God in all three areas of our being (Rom. 1:24, 26, 28). So our response of faith is a mental, emotional, and physical response to the grace of God.

Faith in God's displeasure with our sin causes the mental response of repentance. Faith in God's action of sending his Son causes our hearts to cry out for cleansed emotions in our faith-admission (confession) of the sonship of Jesus. Faith in God's saving action at the cross and open tomb causes us to respond in the faith-encounter of baptism. Appreciative and appropriate faith is that total response of the total person to the grace of God.

We Are His Product (2:9-10)

"Not of works," Paul reminds us. Pride in our own works leads to bragging or lack of gratefulness to God. Paul says no human activity can add to the merits of the cross. Nothing we do, no matter how great or praiseworthy, can add to the virtue of Jesus' death for us. The human response called for is faith, faith in what God has done and will do. Faith accepts the merits of the cross. Faith is never merely contemplative or intellectual. Faith causes us to identify with the cross in repentance and baptism.

Repentance and baptism are not additions to faith, but they are faith in action claiming the benefits of the cross and open tomb. Out of this comes God's product — a new man created to work for God out of joyous gratitude for God's gracious salvation.

We work because we are his. We are his "workmanship" (literally, we are his *poiema* — his poem). This means we are not self-made. As Christians we are God-made, and that is the determining factor in our personal and community lives. We do not work to gain his acceptance. We work because he has already accepted us in Christ (Rom. 5:6-11).

Of course, if we do not work we indicate we have not rightly understood the nature of our salvation (James 2:14-17). Inactivity and discipleship are not compatible. We practice these good actions as a normal expression of daily faith in God, who has worked so many wonderful things for us in Christ.

We work because our Father works. If our good works result in conversions, we rejoice in more of God's grace. If we work and people do not respond, we continue to work. We work at the direction of our Father because it is his nature to bless and to help. We work because God trusts us to carry out his actions. The greatest program the church has going for it is when every Christian works for his Father wherever and whenever he can.

41

Strangers 4

When I was in the U.S. Marine Corps I was assigned to the Air Wing in Korea. While on a leave in Japan I stopped in a barbershop to get a shave. I relaxed in the chair, but as the barber shaved my face with his gleaming razor I had a horrible thought: "Less than ten years ago this man was my mortal enemy. He probably would have shot me down on sight, or used this razor to slit my throat." Then with a sigh I realized the war was over. We were strangers no longer. That was good to "remember."

Paul's words in Ephesians 2:11, "Therefore remember . . .," call on the active memory of forgiven and reconciled people (2:11). The Bible often asks us to remember what is important spiritually. Jesus makes the Lord's table more than a fragrant forget-me-not when he asks: "Do this in remembrance of me." Remember what? Remember me! The Lord wants us to remember that it is his sacrifice that is central.

Paul is not playing spiritual "concentration" with his Gentile brethren. Yet, he asks the former pagans never to forget how far they have come in Christ. "Remember constantly (present tense is used) therefore," he says, "the way it used to be with you."[1] Paul does not ask them to dwell on this in a sense of morbid muckraking. Rather, he wants their memories to continue to prod them into constant thankfulness for the undeserved grace of God. They should remember how much power it took to alter their former lives.

Immature Christians often do not look at their former life styles with much regret. Sometimes this immaturity causes them to harbor secret pride about their former conduct. "I used to be a real character," they say with a touch of wistfulness. They act as though the only real distinctiveness about them is what they used to be. Such spiritual infants remain so near the door of their entrance into Christ, they are in constant danger of falling out. If their memory was as accurate as it should be, they would have insight into the horrifying futility of existing apart from Christ. Paul calls upon the memory to strip the past of its romantic daydreams about heroic evil feats. When we remember the sordidness of evil living, we thank God for our present forgiven life.

The Monotonous Life (2:11)

There was nothing compelling or romantically interesting about the Gentile's former existence (2:11-12). Evil people do not know more than good people, nor are their lives more interesting or vital. Evil people are not more fun to be around, nor are

43

they really sophisticated. There is a sameness about an evil life that is monotonously unoriginal.

What experiences have carnal people had with life's near-overpowering temptations? What do they know about true regret caused by realizing so much time and energy has been wasted in self-service? Have they experienced the yearning to be holier and more useful in the service of God? Where has their struggle to do right instead of wrong taken them? Have they continued to wallow in self-pity and self-aggrandizement? Hasn't temptation often meant an opportunity to quit the struggle? People who remain in evil are naive and inexperienced.

People who remember who and what they were without Christ know the power of evil. They have no romantic illusions about life apart from God. Recognition of the hideous realities of this agonizing separation grips them. They know what it is to be lost — and to be saved. They recall vividly the horror of being mastered by malignant forces. The degrading effects of such a life holds no charms. Redeemed and alive in Christ, they are the most interesting and knowledgeable people.

Hopeless Strangers (2:12-13)

The former pagan remembers how serious his predicament was apart from Christ: "Separated from Christ, alienated from the commonwealth of Israel, a stranger to the covenants of promise, having no hope and without God in the world" (2:12).[1] But now! Yes, Paul uses the emphatic "now." "At this very moment," he affirms, "you who were at one time far away have become near by means of the blood of

Christ" (2:13)[1] What a difference the blood of Christ makes. What could never be achieved by willpower, headpower, or manpower is achieved by cross-power. Nothing so radically renovates our character and status like the blood of the cross.

The phrase "separate from Christ" expresses desolation. Paul does not mention "apart from Christ" as merely one of a series of spiritually deficient states. Being apart from Christ isolates a person from every spiritual blessing. To miss Christ is to miss all God's riches.

Being apart from Christ also means alienation from citizenship in Israel. An alien is a stranger, an outcast. Serving God is an alien experience to the sinful outsider. Without Christ he can never know the privilege of being part of God's chosen people. Citizenship in Israel does not refer to the land, but to our right of access to God.

Wandering Strangers

The words alienation and stranger describe our modern world very well. Some of the best thinkers of our day sense this estrangement. "The deepest need of man," one of them says, "is the need to overcome his separation, to leave the prison of his aloneness." Another echoes this sentiment in different words: We are . . . "out of touch, avoiding close relationships, having an inability to feel." In other words, we are going it alone, without God and without closeness to what matters. Our alienation from God might be more bearable if we had each other, but our distance from God has also caused a

45

great gulf in our dealings with our fellow man. We are strangers.

Alienated people today do not live and let live. Miserable themselves, they are experts at spreading their misery to others. The destructive acts of modern-day anarchists bear vicious witness to their increasingly desperate mood. Violence pours from our newspapers and television screens upon the unshaped minds of our youth. Alienation breeds alienation.

Man is unable to make or sustain healthy human relationships. All is sex, or violence, or manipulation, or buy-buy-buy consumership. The current virus of polarization between young and old, black and white, student and worker, parent and child, man and woman indicates the depth of this estrangement. As Pogo, the comic strip possum, said: "We have met the enemy, and he is us."

Is there no solution to this alienation? Not as long as we are adrift. An outcast knows no peace until he is home again. To refuse to face the spiritual facts of life is to condemn ourselves to a perpetual life of being a "stranger" to God and to one another.

Hope Is Sure

Not only does our alienation make us outcasts, it also robs us of any meaningful hope (2:12). Loss of hope causes a real sense of despair and futility. Once, a man lost in a snowstorm died in his own backyard. He had given up hope of getting home. A bleak but accurate picture of modern man.

Apart from Christ we only press our nose against the pane and look in from the outside. Like hungry men without a penny peering into some fine eating place, we enjoy no entrance or satisfaction. Christ comes along, though, and escorts us into the company of the privileged diners. They are forgiven sinners, as helpless without Christ as we. The difference? Accepting the help and hope that come from Christ.

The promises of God assure us of help and hope. Hope in the Bible does not mean wishful thinking; it means confident expectation. We hope because God is the source of real hope. If someone asks you if you are saved, you might reply: "I hope so." The Bible does not use hope in that way. Hope in the Bible means total reliance on what God has already done. Hope is not based on whatever you and I can humanly expect. Hope is sure.

"Hope in the Bible means total reliance on what God has already done."

Hope, of course, must be realistic. God offers real hope to us. Albert Speer, Nazi minister of armaments in World War II, wrote in his memoirs about his "hopes" for an early release from Spandau Prison. He was sentenced by the Allies to serve twenty years. He kept hearing rumors that his sentence would be shortened and he would soon be released. But nothing came of it. He served his complete sentence. All his hopes were variously concocted opinions without real grounds. Man without God has no solid basis for hope.

God and hope go together: "May the God of hope fill you with all joy and peace in believing so that by the power of the Holy Spirit you may abound in hope" (Rom. 15:13).[1] God is the source of hope. His concrete acts in history convince us we can rely on his serious commitment to our spiritual well-being.

Hope Is Now

God gives us hope for a future worth having. He inspires us with a sense of well-being about our essential personal survival. God is there. God will continue to be there. Those who focus on man are sure to despair. People who focus on God do not depend on what is humanly possible.

Hope is now. Not just in the future, but now. Your new life is now. Your reconciliation and oneness in Christ are now. Christ is not merely going to act in our future, Christ acts now. Your former self — the stranger — no longer exists. Christ has bridged the gap between you and God. You are no longer strangers. God has worked in your life and converted you to a new humanity.

First Corinthians 6:9-11 illustrates how God takes raw material and makes something valuable of it. Thieves, sexual deviates, and big mouths are potential material for God to use to build up his spiritual temple. God recycles human garbage to make it acceptable and useful. It's not what a man was, it's what he can become. Our wretched spiritual poverty encounters the lavish grace of God, and we are now at peace with him. And our relationship is now no longer one of long-distance. We are in his very presence (2:13). We have true riches.

48

One in Christ (2:14-15)

If the classic case of alienation between Jew and Gentile could be healed, any rift is capable of being closed in Christ. A prominent Rabbi was purportedly asked what God had in mind in creating so many Gentiles. He is reported to have replied: "So there might be fuel enough for the fires of Gehenna." Gentiles could be just as abrasive. During the intertestamental period they tried to eradicate or assimilate the Jewish culture. Our own times have also seen racial hatred carried to extremes. Hitler resurrected the issue in our century by fueling fires with European Jews.

Who can end this hostility? No statesman has accomplished it. No human negotiations have established peace to heal broken relationships. Instead, "he himself is our peace . . ." (2:14).[1] "He made both one and destroyed the intervening barrier . . ." Christ is our peacemaker. We do not get along with our fellow Christians because we are so personable or noble. We accept them as we have been accepted by Christ. We must keep the peace because it is a fundamental denial of Christ's work to allow gaps and barriers to develop between his people. The true church includes all reconciled people.

Paul uses a bold physical figure when he speaks of the removal of the barrier between alienated persons. He probably had in mind the warning signs posted around the Jerusalem temple. Scholars have unearthed two of these signs. The text of one says:

"Let no foreigners venture to enter the enclo-
sure around the Temple. Whoever shall be

49

caught will be the cause of his own death which will follow."

This barrier to fellowship was "a spiritual Berlin wall." Walls between people isolate the church. How can there ever be oneness? God acts in his people to show the world that oneness is possible. God's pilot project is the church where Christ is accomplishing peace. Actually oneness is already here — in Christ! We must rely on his work of oneness and accept its reality. We must agree to accept the centrality of Christ's work in our lives. We may not agree on fringe subjects, but we must accept what is at the center. We will ultimately agree because we agree with Christ!

The War Is Over

In Christ the war is over. Hostilities are ended. And it is not the peace of some shaky armistice, but a true end to hostilities. To do this Jesus personally ended the possibility of justification by law. As long as Jews had the law they could point at the Gentiles and say: "This separates us." But Christ has shown that justification by the law is impossible. Only one man kept the law, and that was Christ. Christ, therefore, robs any man of his boast to be different because of the law.

All will be justified by Christ, or they will not be justified at all. If all are justified by Christ, then all are dependent upon Christ and not the law. The law serves as an admirable sign post to show how far men are from justification. Only in the cross can men draw near to God.

While I was stationed in Korea, the Armistice was signed and there was to be peace in the land. But there was no real peace. Barriers were still up. Sniping and killing continued. The armistice was in name only. The church must not be characterized by continual skirmishes. Grace must reign there. We must remember to point our weapons, not at each other, but at the real enemy, Satan. Think how tremendous it is when harried, harrassed people find a group bound together in the peace of Christ.

Christ and the Body (2:16)

Christ died to reconcile strangers into one body (2:16). There must be one body or reconciliation is a farce. Our ideas of the body, the church, must surrender to God's plans for this unified relationship. Reconciliation is not merely from man to God, but also from man to man. That is the function of the body. It is a relationship of reconciled men and women. It is not enough to claim reconciliation. The cross of Jesus has a two-fold purpose.

In this section Paul focuses on the activity of Christ. Stand aside and see the accomplishments of Christ! Open your hearts and lives to grace. We must have a heart for grace, a capacity to appreciate the actions of Christ. Christ has:

  −Caused us to be able to draw near to God.
  −Made peace between warring men.
  −Destroyed the barriers that separate us.
  −Nullified the law as a justifying principle.
  −Created the new man in himself.
  −Reconciled men to God and to each other.
  −Caused us to grow up as God's family.

The Double Reconciliation (2:16-17)

Paul employs one of the great biblical terms when he speaks of Christ's reconciling work. "Reconciliation" means the re-establishment of a relationship. The Bible nowhere speaks of men reconciling themselves to God. Instead, God causes reconciliation. God restores broken relationships.

In 2 Corinthians 5:18-21, Paul places emphasis on God's outreach: "God was in Christ reconciling the world unto himself, not counting their misdeeds to their account, and placing with us the ministry of reconciliation."[1] We are called to accept God's reconciling action. Truly God has come in the person of Jesus Christ in search of lost sheep.

We may take a hasty look at passages like this and decide: "This is great, I wouldn't mind being reconciled to God." However, we must not think that reconciliation is a one-on-one relationship with God alone. We must not think that God is great, but dismiss his people. We cannot talk of worshipping God out on some mountainside, all by ourselves, or say: "Give me God, but keep the church." This indicates an acceptance of only half of what Jesus died for. At the cross God not only reached out to reconcile man to Himself, but also to reconcile man to man.

Strangers No Longer (2:18-19)

Have you ever been introduced to a famous person? The President of the U.S.? You would want that introduction handled right, wouldn't you? Well, Paul indicates a wonderful thing has happened to the Christian. He has been introduced by Christ, not just

52

to some political figure, but to the creator of the universe. Our introduction to God was more than just a "how are you?" or a passing handshake. We now have "access" to an ongoing relationship.

The word "access" (in Greek *prosagoge*) has an interesting history (2:18). In Xenophon, a contemporary of Socrates, the word is used of foreign ambassadors being introduced into the presence of the Great King of Persia. No one could come unannounced into that royal presence! And we can not just pop in to see God. Someone must introduce us. Someone has! Jesus has introduced us to the Father!

Metaphors are not always big enough to explain all that God is doing for us. Paul uses the comparisons of a body, a family, and a building to help us understand. Our altered relationship with God and each other has made us members of a body (2:16), fellow citizens with God's holy people (2:19), and members of God's family (2:19).

We're in the family! If your family is not precious to you, you do have problems. Most of us want to spend as much time as possible with our family. We belong! When my family gathers I never say: "Why should I be a part of that gathering?" That's my family, and I wouldn't miss the get-togethers for anything. How our ideas of loyalty to the church would be transformed if we saw the church as God's family, and acted accordingly.

A Dwelling Place (2:20-22)

This family is also a temple, or a sanctuary. A sanctuary is where God dwells. God formerly dwelt

53

in the tabernacle and then in the temple in Jerusalem. Now he dwells in the midst of his people. He is no long-distance God. He is near. We are actually living stones in a great spiritual structure. Every brick is important to the Builder. Even the former strangers are part of the structure (2:22).

This is a remarkable building. It grows, and we grow with it. To be in God and to have God in us is to be always growing. What does not grow, dies. God wants no status quo disciples who have no desire to grow and expand in their faith.

This wonderful structure is possible because of its foundation. God had chosen certain men, apostles and prophets, as a foundation ministry (2:20). The foundation ministers testified to a unique event, the Christ-event. They placed Him as the resolute cornerstone to God's structure. Their message is the perpetual basis for a true relationship with God. Why? Because it is the message of the eternally valid work of the Christ on the cross who emerged from the tomb.

This message can be told, but not altered. It can be expounded, but not replaced. Why? Because it is the definitive answer to the largest problem man ever faces, his sinful estrangement from God. To try and update this message is to attempt to alter the basic manner of God's dealing with sin. Response to this message takes the "stranger" into God's dwelling. That can never change. Thank God!

Mystery 5

Man has an insatiable appetite for mystery. Suspense seasons his reading, viewing, and imagination. The Christian, however, is intensely absorbed in a mystery unique from all others. It begins with a promise of great riches.

How would you like to be told you are heir to a treasure so vast, so incomprehensible, that it is called "unsearchable?" Well, you are if you are in Christ (3:8). What once was a mystery has now been revealed (3:3). Paul tells in this section about his great privilege of announcing this good news to potential heirs. Paul found out, as we will also when we share it, that news of a revealed mystery travels fast!

Paul writes with assurance that the Gentiles had now discovered the open secret of riches in Christ. He also shares with his readers a commitment to the great cause that is so dear to him. He declares his joy in proclaiming God's far-reaching purpose for all men. Because of this, even though a prisoner, he asks them to reflect on the glory of such a ministry (3:13).

The Great Because (3:1-2)

"Because of this . . . "[1] Some great *because* should stand at the heart of each man's life. Because of all that has been said. Because God has acted in Christ to put people back together again. Because God has placed reconciled people in one body. Because God has extended grace to all those dead in sin. Because the great foundation is forever established and men and women can be built up in God's spiritual temple. Because! This is a because to be reckoned with. This because is a cause, a great cause and ministry.

What is man without a great cause, a great adventure? God does not invite men to play dull spiritual charades. He calls them to a great cause. To burn brightly on the winds of time as shining beacons of grace in operation. How heretical to make a bore of Christianity! Though a prisoner Paul can point to the great "because" of his life. It meant that grace was operating.

Grace is the great "because." Paul hopes the Gentiles know the appropriate response to that compelling "because." It is a responsibility to tell about grace. The word translated as "dispensation" or "stewardship" (*oikonomia*) speaks of responsibility (3:2) — a person being entrusted with something greater than himself. He is called to act responsibly with it, administering it for the benefit of the owner (1 Cor. 9:17). Paul says in 1 Timothy 1:11

that he was "entrusted with the glorious gospel of the blessed God."[1] This idea conveys the tremendous concept of being trusted by God.

Can we be trusted? God thinks so. His grace calls us into a relationship of trust. How disloyal it would be to violate God's trust. A man, seated at a banquet, introduced himself to his neighbor, who turned out to be the president of the local bank. "Oh," said the first man, "I know Mr. _____ who works for you. I'm sure he is a trusted and tried employee." The bank president scowled in reply: "He was trusted and he'll be tried as soon as he's caught." We must prove worthy of our trust.

What was entrusted to Paul? Some esoteric insights so intricate that they could only be felt and not shared? Not at all! He was trusted with a glorious ministry that would inform the despised Gentiles of God's gracious purpose for them. Strange that this one man, who had placed such pride in his race, his attainments, his pedigrees, should be the instrument of announcing God's mercy to the outcasts. The humbling realization that all men, Jews and Gentiles, needed the forgiving grace of God did wonders for Paul's attitude. It can do the same for us.

Making Sense of Mystery (3:3-4)

There is a mystery about all this. What can it mean? The mystery is this: God has acted to accept all men who will to know him. The gospel is divine information, not human. Paul's use of the word "mystery" (*mysterion*) should not cause us to think of a who-done-it (3:3). Mystery here means an "open

57

secret," a great hidden fact now open to those willing and eager to learn. This mystery is not some exclusive, cryptic insight for the know-it-all elite. It is the great good news that a Savior is available. This is God's great insight, and to this we must respond. Salvation is not earned by mastering some difficult bits of information, but by depending upon the one whom God has revealed.

"Revelation," or unveiling of his will, by God benefits those needing rescue from their sins. Revelation is not subjective. Christianity is not an experience-gathering excursion, but dependence upon God. Revelation is not the result of man's mental assaults upon the gates of heaven. It is the life-giving Word from God.

Revelation is God's own information about Christ. What could we possibly add to this? What could possibly be more significant than this? These acts of our Lord are the basis of all apostolic preaching. The apostles did not preach their own experiences, but the life-giving word of God, which alone has the power to save.

Paul's readers also can understand the apostolic insight (3:4). Revelation can be rationally understood. This message calls for perception, not emotion. Emotion will come when we are intellectually overwhelmed by the magnitude of God's grace. We will feel good because we will know we have been pardoned and have made a faith response to the gospel. The gospel, a message from God, makes sense.

The biblical view of man is emphasized here. Man is capable of responding rationally and understanding the gospel. He can make the right response if he listens to the right information. Right thinking leads to right conclusions. This is good information to keep in mind in today's climate of irrationality.

The New Nonsense

We live in the era of the "new nonsense," one modern writer claims. Apparently, he means there is more *non*sense around today than ever before. More students study astrology than astronomy in our colleges today. People choose all kinds of mind-blowing experiences. Even the Holy Spirit is supposedly behind this new irrationality, according to some. He purportedly picks the pronunciation of irrational sounds as a sure sign of His presence! Have we forgotten that we are to love the Lord our God with our minds as well as with our hearts?

"The mystery is this: God has acted to accept all men who will to know him."

The essential feature of heathen revelation in apostolic times was its irrationality. The oracle at Delphi spoke from a frenzy, the priestess supposedly mastered by Apollo. The ancients thought the best poetry and insights came from madmen. The words for maniac and spontaneous prophesy are related in Greek. Horace, the sage Roman poet, cautioned against listening to a poet in a stupor of *divine madness (Arts Poetica)*. It was this sort of irrational view of man that the gospel spoke against.

It was no accident when Paul cast out the evil spirit from the young girl in Philippi (Acts 16). That spirit has been identified as a Pythian spirit, the very force motivating the irrational oracle of Delphi. Euripides, in his play the *Bacchae*, seems to counsel that man can combine rationality and irrationality and live with it. But this is foreign to the spirit of the biblical view of man and God.

All of this does not mean that our reason is so powerful that we can think our way through to God unaided. We cannot obtain insight into God's mind by human wisdom. God does not lie at the end of a syllogism. The best logicians do not necessarily make the best Christians. Still, the information God provides is valid. Reasonable men can respond to it with understanding. Existence is not absurd. There is ultimate meaning and ultimate truth. God desires for us to know him. His message can be communicated, understood, and we can respond.

Claiming Promises (3:5-6)

Knowing God and Christ is possible. All people have not always been privileged to know of God's plans (3:5). The foundation ministry (apostles and New Testament prophets) testified to those unalterable historical events about Christ which give a sure basis for faith.

This foundation ministry also reveals that there are no second-class citizens in the kingdom of God. All who are converted share the same spiritual benefits (3:5-6). Gentiles share as heirs, members of the body of Christ, and partners in the promises.

Sharing is the essence of God's nature. He does not hoard. When we learn to be generous, we are learning to be like our heavenly Father. Our share in the faith is bountiful indeed:

Sharing the inheritance — We are not hired hands, but members of the family. We share a full portion.

Sharing in the body — We do not have a trial membership, but a full, functional relationship with the Head. We are just as important as anybody, and just as useful.

Sharing in the promises — Peter tells the repentant sinners who are baptized into Jesus Christ that "the promise of the Spirit is for them, their children, all who are far off, even as many as the Lord our God shall call" (Acts 2:39).[1] God does not intend to shortchange anybody. No one trusting in God will be left with his nose pressed against the windowpane of heaven looking in from the outside.

Anyone who travels with God travels first class all the way. What a shame that so many Christians take the ship of faith and are willing to go third-class.

A story is told about a man who saved money to make an ocean voyage. He thought he could help save by preparing his own meals, so he brought along a large supply of cheese and crackers for the trip. On the ship, while luscious meals were being served on the dining deck, this man munched his cheese and crackers down below. Finally, on the last day, he became disgusted with cheese and crackers and asked about the price of one regular meal. "Why there is no extra charge, sir," the dining steward replied, "the meals are all included in the fare." This man had a first class ticket but chose to go in steerage. Too many disciples today fail to realize that Jesus bought a first-class ticket for them!

Unsearchable Riches (3:7-8)

God's power gave a ministry to a man who did not deserve it (3:7-8). And it is the same with each of us. Grace puts man in perspective. Paul does not call himself "the very least of God's dedicated people" merely as a verbal put-down to win sympathy. He was not fishing for compliments. Grace had helped him to put himself into perspective.

Paul's qualifications were from God. They were "given" (3:7). Sometimes well-meaning disciples will say of some person: "What a great member of the body he would make." While some people may be well-qualified from a human point of view, these qualifications do not necessarily commend him to God. God looks on the heart. The ground is level at the foot of the cross. All stand in absolute need of redeeming grace. In this spirit, Paul recognizes that announcing the riches of Christ is by divine privilege, not human qualification.

"For know the grace of our Lord Jesus Christ, that though he was rich, yet for your sake he became poor, so that by his poverty you might become rich" (2 Cor. 8:9).[1] Christ's riches are unsearchable, Paul says (3:8). He uses a remarkable word to describe these riches. They cannot be "tracked out." No one knows the boundaries of the riches of Christ. They are lavish and unending.

Christ's blessings are not doled out with a shallow dipper. No adequate description or list can encompass their vastness. When Howard Hughes was living, people often speculated on his riches. Quite a few "wills" were discovered by people who hoped to receive a generous slice of Hughes' riches. But research discovered that Hughes was not so rich after all. Public imagination had run wild again. There wasn't enough to go around to meet all claims. With Jesus, there is always more than enough to go around. Our God is a living God.

Wisdom in the Mystery (3:9-11)

Not only does Paul relate the riches of Christ, he also reveals God's mystery-plan for the church (3:9-11). Here the word *oikonomia*, which in verse 2 meant "responsibility," apparently means "plan or arrangement." God's mystery — now an open secret — is revealed in an enlightening plan. Now it can be told! If you are in the church you are part of God's well-conceived plan. The church is God's pilot project of the great unity to come. The church demonstrates that God can bring people together. The chaos of sin and darkness does not have to dominate our world and our lives. The church is God's mystery plan.

It is important to note what Paul is saying in verse 10. He is not saying the church is being proclaimed as an object of faith to men on earth. Nor does he say *here* that the church is the agent proclaiming God's wonderful wisdom, as true as that may be. He is saying that the church as an entity created by God reflects God's many-sided wisdom to the unseen powers. These powers, apparently the hostile forces discussed in Ephesians 6:12, are confronted with an established fact — the church.

God shows that reconciliation between God and man — and man and man — is possible. The evidence he presents is the church. Hostile forces stand against any sort of unity. They fight against reconciliation and oneness. They divide and antagonize men against each other. They obscure the newly revealed secret. However, when they see God's church, they are confounded by his wisdom, and they know that oneness is possible.

Living in the Heavenlies

The phrase "in the heavenlies" is essentially the same word translated as heaven in many places in the New Testament. In Ephesians, however, it is a plural adjective with the Greek preposition *epi* as a prefix. First, Paul says God has blessed us with every spiritual blessing in the heavenlies in Christ (1:20). He then brings us the amazing news that those in Christ have been raised together with Christ (past tense) and have been caused to sit together with Christ (past tense) in the heavenlies (2:6). Then, of course, we have these two references to the hostile spiritual powers (3:10; 6:12).

Obviously, "heavenlies" refers to a spiritual situation. It cannot mean the final heavenly situation where God is experienced directly and evil is expelled forever. We are living and struggling in a heavenly sphere right now. As Christians we are not merely concerned with earthly matters, but we share in heavenly blessings and heavenly concerns now.

Paul asks us to realize that we are currently involved in heavenly matters.

Our relationship with God is not in the future only, but also in the present. There is a final consummation, of course, but we can now possess and enjoy the blessings of God and engage in the struggle against evil. The church stands squarely in the path of those divisive forces that would further alienate and divide mankind. The church stands as a great tribute to God's reconciling power.

"We are living and struggling in a heavenly sphere right now."

A united, loving congregation of God's people is a dynamic demonstration that God's mystery has been revealed. To the forces of hostility and hatred, it is a continued vindication of God's wisdom. We are challenged to let the unity of God reign in our midst.

The church reveals the many sides (3:10) of God's wisdom. The hostile powers could not have expected God to create an island of love and reconciliation in the middle of a sea of hatred. But God always demonstrates the inexhaustible nature of his wisdom.

Evil powers and evil men always underestimate God. They see God through their frame of reference and think he is as limited as they are. We must always beware of spiritual tunnel-vision. The church is not as small as some men imagine, but it is as magnificent as God planned it to be.

God's mystery plan was no last-minute expediency (3:9). The church was no accident of history. Eternal purpose lies behind it (3:11). Christ and his people are the purpose of the ages. Again we see that Christ is not merely another divine avatar, not just another great teacher, not just a good man. He is God's purpose in actual reality.

The wisdom of God can only be vindicated when the church continually holds up Jesus Christ as head and savior. After all, Christ provides our right to be in the presence of God.

Confident before the Father (3:12-13)

Paul declared the wonderful news about our access into God's presence (2:18). To that privilege he adds another treasure given us in Christ, "boldness" (3:12-13). In ancient Athens boldness described a citizen's right to speak out freely in the assembly. Christ does not invite us into the presence of God, then command us to be silent. Instead, we are invited to express our wants and needs. We have the privilege to speak with confidence in God's presence.

Christ's people are confident, but not overconfident. Their confidence and assurance come from faith in Christ, not from themselves. A lack of confidence in our lives reflects a lack of confidence in Christ. I have confidence in my automobile when I know a good mechanic has worked on it. I drive with more confidence when my car has new tires. Why? Because I have confidence in myself? No, because I have confidence in the mechanic and the tires. In the same way, I live confidently as a Christian because I have confidence in Christ's ability to save me.

66

If confidence is missing in our lives, we show that Jesus' action on our behalf has not been very effective. Christ did not come to create fearful, negative people. One mark of the presence of Christ is a confident attitude toward God. You may trust God's work!

No wonder this good news travels so fast. Once announced, an electrifying mystery like this cannot be hidden. It must be shared. The open secret reveals that what God has done and is doing:

(1) Is good news,
(2) Spreads amazingly fast when the messenger counts it a privilege to share it,
(3) Is a source of unsearchable riches,
(4) Can be understood,
(5) Is for everyone,
(6) Creates confidence, and
(7) IS ABOUT CHRIST!

Power 6

A Christian has the right of bold access to God. Boldness is not arrogance though. A high school teacher of mine used to say: "Familiarity does not breed *contempt*, it breeds *attempt*." Familiarity with something or someone might cause a thoughtless person to try presumptive acts. An electrician, for example, who spends many hours working with high voltage, always reminds himself that the power at his fingertips permits no presumption. We achieve boldness toward God through a continued attitude of respect for his power.

"For this cause I bow my knees . . ." (3:14).[1] This is like saying: "For this cause I pray . . . ." Bowing the knees was a customary sign of submission and respect. New Testament people prayed in all sorts of positions and postures. Paul and Silas even prayed one memorable evening while locked in the Philippi jail. Instead of shouting for their lawyer, they prayed to God. The attitude of the heart, not the posture of the body, is the important thing. Is the heart bowed down before almighty God?

Here Paul prays again. Now a prayer of intercession is on his heart. We can show a mark of concern for others by our willingness to go to the Father on their behalf. Prayer is natural to the Lord's true followers.

Our Father in heaven is not only available, he actually encourages his children to come to him in prayer day or night. Even many well-meaning people say, "Call on us if there's anything we can do." But they usually do not absolutely mean it. After all, they can only fit so many people and so many needs into their schedule. God is not limited. He can fit all of us into his busy schedule.

Fatherhood (3:14-15)

"From whom every fatherhood . . . . "Instead of the father analogy being a way of understanding God, Paul suggests that understanding God is a way of understanding fatherhood. All that is best in the concept of fatherhood appears primarily in God as Father. If today's fathers based their ideas and ideals of fatherhood on God's nature, they would come much closer to knowing the greater realities of being a father.

Jesus spends much time revealing the Father's nature to the human race. Beginning in Luke 15:11 there are several important factors about fatherhood:

1. The father's deep longing for reconciliation with the lost son. Fathers should care.

69

2. The father's expectant outlook and welcome willingness to forgive and restore without question. Fathers should love.
3. The father's deep sense of what is appropriate. Fathers should forgive.

Spiritual Needs

Paul concentrates, as he prays, on the spiritual needs of his readers. He knows they need power to meet these needs. It takes time and effort to know what people's real needs are. We are experts at putting out false needs. Of course, often we do not know our own real needs. A boy might fervently pray for a motorcycle to end his misery. With a motorcycle, he probably would find that he could now motor his misery over a wider area. Still he'd be miserable. Just like false answers, false needs lack power to satisfy.

It usually astounds imperceptive people to find that someone has a need they never suspected. "I thought he had everything to make him happy," they'll say about a suicide. Perhaps they never took the time to know the person's needs. We must put our antennae out and listen. Once a man boasted, "I've been married twenty-four years and never had an argument with my wife." Someone who knew the situation said, "Brother, you just haven't been listening."

Spiritual needs can begin to be satisfied when we awaken to our true needs. Once we become alert, we should pray for what is truly needed. God will answer. Jesus says to "seek first God's kingdom and righteousness." We agree, but it isn't real to us. How

70

can we put it into focus? Only by recognizing the priority of these spiritual needs.

All our gadgets, gimmicks, and achievements leave us with a kingsized yearning in our hearts. They are powerless to satisfy. What satisfaction is there like spiritual satisfaction? Only God can satisfy that deepest of heart-hungers. We remain powerless only as long as we fail to use the power available. His glorious riches come from a never-ending treasury.

Is it strange to speak of God possessing riches? He owns all. We are the impoverished ones. "The earth is mine . . ." is the magnificent theme of Psalms 50.[1] God is rich. Just ask.

Enabling Power (3:16-18)

What is the object of Paul's prayer? He points to a transcending power. Staggering, amazing, yet available to *all* saints (3:18). Paul prays for Christians to be given power so they might be strengthened in the inner person (3:18). "Power" is the Greek *dunamis*. We instantly recognize its connection with our English words dynamite and dynamic.

But what does "power" mean in this verse? The basic idea is "capability," or what we could call "enabling" power.

Paul prays that God's power will unveil all the spiritual resources available to us in Christ. He wants our lives to operate on the basis of a true involvement with the indwelling Christ. This faith will root and ground us in love and give us strength to recognize the astounding love of Christ.

71

Having power means being in touch with boundless spiritual resources. God's power means "God enables." He makes it possible for us to act in a certain way otherwise impossible. God's power in the gospel, for example, makes it possible for my faith-response to result in salvation (Rom. 1:16). Had God not acted to make the gospel available, my response would be meaningless. But as it is, I have God's power for salvation because God made it possible.

"God's power in the gospel makes it possible for my faith-response to result in salvation."

We must *not* think God's power overrides our will and removes us from the control of our actions. God works within us by his power as we willingly get involved with him:

. . . Work out your own salvation with fear and trembling; for God is at work in you, both to will and to work for his good pleasure. (Phil. 2:12-13)

God's power is more than psychological motivation. A person may diet because it makes him look better. A woman may motivate herself to "do her duty" for an aged parent, but secretly she may resent the burden. God's power is different. With God a person finds the right motives. A successful dieter will serve the Lord more zestfully with a healthy body. A daughter will care for her aging parent because of love, not mere duty.

God, then, must open us up and let his strength be applied to our inner person (3:16). Our inner man needs God's reinforcement. So much attention is devoted to the outer person today. Are you fashionable? Wear the right clothes? Use the right mouthwash? Go to the right places? What makes us think it all happens on the outside? Are we crumbling inside while we try to act confident before the world?

Paul prays for the strengthening work of the Holy Spirit. Parallel to this is the thought of Christ dwelling in our hearts by faith (3:17). The verb "dwelling" is intensive, meaning "settle down." Christ needs to settle down and take up permanent residence in our hearts. He must never be a temporary guest — a weekend visitor.

Possession of the Spirit is not a reward for our strength, but a necessary presence for our weakness (Rom. 8:13). Paul says the Spirit helps us in our weakness (Rom. 8:26). We do not earn the Spirit by some brave display of discipleship. He is a gracious gift from God to help gird up what is too weak to survive alone (Eph. 6:14).

Spiritual Shortcuts

In relying on God's power we must be careful not to take spiritual shortcuts. Blazing our own trail of discipleship may cause us to get lost again. Spiritual shortcuts turn into spiritual short-circuits. Looking for the power of God is not an end in and of itself. Simon Magus found this out. His story reveals a man impatient to have the power of God for his own end (Acts 8). He wanted apostolic power, but he did not have apostolic credentials. He desired power to satisfy his own concern, but he had no decent concern for the truth of the gospel. He had not been with Jesus, but he wanted to shortcut it all. Simon ended up with a badly short-circuited Christian life.

We should not give up on the idea of God's power just because some people misuse it. There have always been people who seek only "signs and wonders that they may believe." But such frothy excitement should not cause true believers to avoid the vast spiritual resources the Father makes available.

Jesus needed power when faced with temptation in the wilderness. The devil only wanted a cheap miracle (Matt. 4:1ff), but Jesus refused. The call to take the world from the devil's hand is the same sort of shortcut. The effortless assumption of authority over the kingdoms would have meant that a crown could be won without a cross. That is never the way of Jesus, who chose God's power even though it meant a cross.

An Energy Crisis

The apostles also worked spectacular signs. But they also needed the inner strength Paul talks about here. Without the strength and presence of God no disciple could resist the devil's power. Jesus himself appealed to the Father and scripture as sources of spiritual power in his resistance of the archenemy (Matt. 4:1ff).

The latter part of the twentieth century is noted for crises. Everything seems to be running out. Our natural resources are abused at a reckless rate.

The possibility of freezing in the dark confronts the world.

As bad as these natural crises are, they are insignificant considering man's lack of spiritual power. An endless supply of spiritual power is available. Spiritual power is not the ability to play slick mystical tricks or the search for self-exalting experiences. We need the power to make our lives a meaningful blessing to ourselves, others, and our God. The power we need enables us to become what we should become.

We need the power that comes from living daily in a close relationship with God; the power to reach out to others in such a way that they learn to depend, not on us, but God, the power to break destructive habits and behavior, to love the unlovable, to adventure out on the broken pavement of life's highway, to rescue crushed and perplexed people from despair (2 Cor. 4:7-18).

Without God's power we are trying to get by on our own resources. We become weary in well-doing without much well-doing. Without a connection to the power source our batteries quickly wear down. Worn-out batteries can be dangerous. They corrode and leak acid. A powerless Christian is a tribute to the devil's power to drain batteries. We need a permanent connection to the power of God.

Power is maintained in prayer, in reading and living the word, in closeness to our brethren. Even a nuclear-powered submarine can only go so long on its own. We can do nothing without God. "Apart from me you do not have the ability to do even one thing" (John 15:5).[1]

75

Transplanted and Renovated (3:17)

Paul describes our life in the power of God. We are firmly rooted and based in love. The participles in this verse are perfect, which in Greek means that we have been rooted and are still rooted in love. We have been given a foundation in love and are still in the foundation. This is true as long as Christ dwells in our hearts by faith.

Love is the soil in which the Christian is rooted. Love is the foundation upon which our lives rest. You have been transplanted from non-productive, barren soil to good soil. Growth is possible. Roses do not grow in the desert. If we are not growing in Christ, we need to check the soil in which we are rooted, or see if we are rooted at all.

Our foundation is love, which forms a solid basis for building a new life. Christ has torn down our former life, a miserable little shack. In its place he has erected a building on the solid rock of love. When you call upon Christ to do a rebuilding job, he doesn't just paint or redecorate. He renovates the structure right down to the foundation.

Do You Get It? (3:18)

Paul continues his prayer so we might have the strength to grasp, with all the dedicated ones (saints), the dimensions of God's love for us in Christ (3:18). The verb translated "grasp" is *katalambano*. It appears in John 1:5: "the darkness does not 'master' the light."[1] Two meanings are possible: to master physically and to master intellectually. John probably intends both meanings here.

76

The darkness cannot "extinguish" the light, but neither can it "understand" it. The verb here can also have these two meanings. We should pray for strength, as Paul does, to grasp the love of Christ as a direct benefit for our lives. We should also pray to grasp the meaning of this all-powerful love. Another way of asking the question might be: Are you getting his love into your life, and do you grasp it?

Paul prays for "all the saints" to grasp the love of Christ. Too many religious and philosophical movements have attempted to promote the egos of an "enlightened" elite. People like this in Paul's time were called gnostics, a religious "know-it-all" who believed salvation came from an exclusive knowledge of certain esoteric propositions rather than by surrendering to God in faith. The gnostic believed he possessed the key to knowledge denied to ordinary disciples. New Testament writers fight hard against this deviation. Jesus did not die for a handful of elite. He died for each of us, brilliant and ignorant alike. The whole church must and can grasp Christ's revolutionary love. May we never think only a handful of Christians are going to "get it."

Knowing the Unknowable (3:19)

How do you know what is beyond knowing? We cannot fully comprehend Christ's love for us. We cannot master the dimensions of it. But we can know he loves us! That much we can grasp. The cross points to it. The cross is a concrete demonstration in history of Christ's limitless love. We know he loves us, even if we never completely understand it.

A literalist has trouble with passages like these. We understand a mother when she writes her three sons in three different cities and sends "all her love." Some literalist might insist that *all* her love would have been exhausted with the first greeting, but the hearts of her sons know better. They know she loves them. She has demonstrated it. We cannot analyze Christ's love in a chemical laboratory, but we can know it and depend on it. Christ's love for us is designed to produce fullness. The fullness of God is being developed, filled-out, into the outlines God has planned for us. Christ's love is creative, not stagnant. Christ wants us to grow to completeness. Disciples who have stopped growing frustrate God's plan for them. We should beware of stopping at some spiritual dead-end.

Spiritual Dead-ends

For years our family traveled an interstate highway which ended in a cotton patch. We had to take a bumpy old road for miles and miles because one county wouldn't finish its section of the highway. Spiritual dead-ends are much more serious, of course. We start out well enough. A brave beginning. But we get off the main road. Our lives are stagnated in apathy.

There is a saying: "Blessed is he who is going nowhere, for he is sure of his destination." That is the life of people without the love of Christ as a continuing experience of grace.

Dead-ends are littered with people who think they are still traveling. Often we get on the road, then confuse that with arriving. Our small achievement has created a grand illusion that inhibits growth. We think we've already arrived when we stop expecting wonderful things from our relationship with Christ. When we accept where we are as the final destination we severely retard our spiritual growth in Christ. Since Jesus is the way, we must continuously travel. Jesus' road is never dull like dead-ends.

To Him Who Is Able (3:20-21)

God is able (3:20-21). God's power makes us able. If we have any ability to grasp these vital spiritual truths, it is because God makes it possible (3:16). What would we believe in if God had not acted to send Christ and his word?

Paul's benediction says God is able to do "beyond what we ask or think" (3:20).[1] Human attainments are limited. Paul cautions us to examine our limitations and discover they are not God's. We fail because we are afraid. We fear consequences. We have limited vision. We lack dedication.

We are limited, but God is not. When you plan with God, make big plans. Paul says God's ability is the power which works in us (3:20). The present participle stresses that God's power continues to work in us (Col. 1:11). What is it that we may ask? What is it that we may think? If it agrees with God's will, there are no limitations. This prayer could be read with profit at every meeting of church leaders.

Do you worry about giving God such a blank check for your life? Don't worry, God is not capricious. His will is not arbitrary nor whimsical. His power will develop you into what you should be. Don't try and hold God down. He will open doors of opportunity for you to grow and reach out with your faith.

Glory in the Church (3:21)

Paul sets the stage for his great discussion of the body of Christ by calling attention to God's glory which can be seen in Christ and the church. God's glory means all that makes God great. God's true greatness is seen in what he is doing with a body of believers. Paul maintains an exalted view of the church in all his letters.

In our time it's popular to criticize the church. But when this criticism is examined, it is often directed at some deviation from Christ's plan. People should not give up on God's glory in the church because some spurious religious activities are going on. Counterfeit money is circulating — does that mean no real money is around?

Paul never disconnects the church from Christ. Glory is reflected upon God in the church and in Christ Jesus (3:21). These two are inseparable: Christ and the church. The church is God's idea, God's creation. The church is not a historical anachronism, not a haunt for sectarian minds, not a society of pious frauds. It is an instrument for the glory of God. There is power in the body of Christ.

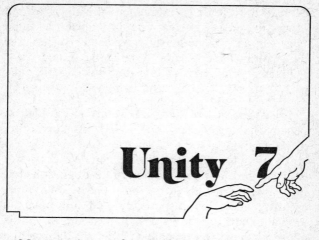

Unity 7

Most students of Ephesians divide it into two parts. The first three chapters are usually styled doctrinal and the last three practical. Although there is some accuracy to this view, Paul would admit no possible separation of doctrine and life. They are all of one piece. Doctrine gives you right ideas about God and your fellow man. Carrying true ideas out in your daily life naturally follows learning doctrine. Paul says, "I encourage you . . . walk worthily of the calling with which you were called" (4:1).[1]

Our Daily Walk (4:1)

"Walk," as used here, is an ethical term. In its simplist form the verb means to walk around (Greek *peripatein*).

A philosophical school, supposedly headed by Aristotle, was established in Athens in the fourth century B.C. Students in the school walked around discussing ideas. So this school received the name "peripatetic." From this the word came to mean "the daily conduct of one's life." Our walk is our conduct. Paul uses "walk" throughout the book of Ephesians (2:2, 2:10, 4:1, 4:17, 5:2, 5:8, and 5:15).

Since God has "called" us, we are in the highest possible calling (2 Thess. 2:13-14). It is an invitation to noble living. God's call is the best and highest motivation for our ethical conduct. We have not been invited into some second-rate operation, but into a relationship with God himself. We must conduct ourselves responsibly and not have an apathetic attitude toward our position as God's chosen people. Irresponsible Christians damage the Lord's cause.

While I served in the U.S. Marine Corps, we had a saying that it was always the "Ten Percent" who fouled everything up. As a result, all the Marines would be blamed. A Marine would go into town, get drunk, smash up his car, and get into trouble with the authorities. People in town would say, "All Marines are troublesome drunks." The "Ten Percent" gave other Marines a bad name.

In the same way, a small minority of saints who fail to perceive the nobility of their "calling" often give the whole church a bad name. Some people are just looking for such excuses, of course, to rationalize about their own failure to "walk worthily of their calling." Still, Paul would not have us give them any opportunity. Live as a city set on a hill, glorifying your Father in heaven (Matt. 5:13-16).

Put Up with One Another (4:2)

The perceptive disciple is aware of the need to give his best. Paul gives some helpful guidelines for developing an attitude which will help us in our worthy walk (4:2). These attitudes primarily center on getting along with our fellow believers. That's where it has to start. After all, if we cannot live peacefully with other followers of the Lord, how can we bring peace and reconciliation to the world?

Our mental attitudes have much to do with good relationships. We can "put up with one another in love" by having "all humility in attitude and gentleness along with long-lasting endurance" (4:2).[1] Paul says we will need *all* the right attitudes we can get to put up with our brothers.

Right attitudes help us in "forbearing" or putting up with each other (4:2). This is not the language we expect — "putting up." Yet, we all recognize how true it is. Jesus used this same word in Matthew 17:17 when he cried out in the presence of his always-slow-to-learn disciples: "O faithless and perverse generation, how long am I to be with you? How long am I to bear (put up) with you?" We rejoice that Jesus did put up with them and with us! Jesus puts up with us because he has the right attitude — love.

Love causes us to go beyond merely enduring our brothers and sisters. We grow into active love for them despite their faults and they in spite of ours. Who would want his wife or husband to say after twenty years of marriage: "I just put up with him." Hopefully, love will have developed the relationship to a higher plane than that. But if we can in love "put up with" extra-sensitive, eccentric, even hard-headed brethren, we may grow into loving them. On the other hand, those of us who tend to be eccentric, sensitive, or opinionated need to work on these problems. The attitudes Paul mentions here are just right to help us in our daily walk.

Unity of the Spirit (4:3)

Our continued worthy walk involves certain duties. When we change our attitudes toward others, we will find we can put up with them. They also may discover that with love they can put up with us. Growing out of this mutual acceptance is a real desire to see unity. We recognize that we are one because the Spirit has given us unity.

We have not achieved unity ("the quality of being one"). The origin of unity is the Spirit. The Spirit put us together into one body. "For by one Spirit we were all baptized into one body" (1 Cor. 12:13). It's the Lord who adds saved people to his body (Acts 2:47). Oneness is a product of the Lord's work, not man's. We are together because we have all affirmed that the Lord is the center in our lives.

We did not create this oneness, but we are encouraged to maintain it. Our duty is to live out a maintenance ministry on behalf of the Spirit's unity. This unity can be shattered by factional people. Some bogus Christians think very little of fragmenting the Spirit's unity. As long as their opinion or idea gains notoriety, they are willing to split the body at the drop of a syllogism. The pride and insolence of such people is frightening. The unity they so thoughtlessly subvert is the Lord's unity created on the cross.

You enlist in some outfits — the Army or Marine Corps. Some ask you to join, saying you can add much to their membership. A fraternity or sorority may "rush" you for your "virtues" or money or good grades. But, you come to the church with no human qualifications for participation, only needs. By maintaining the Spirit's unity we are assured that the church will remain what God wishes for it to be . . . a body functioning to promote growth in grace.

The Seven Ones (4:4-6)

Next Paul mentions seven basic realities. To commit oneself to these facts necessarily leads to unity. Each fact, whether a person of the Godhead or a spiritual quality, testifies to oneness. The fact that verses three to six are one sentence in the original is occasionally obscured in some translations, particularly when verse four begins: "There is one body . . ." "There is" does not exist in the original. Translators insert it to make the sentence seem clearer. A somewhat literal translation actually makes the point clearer:

I encourage you then, I the prisoner in the Lord, that you walk worthily of the calling by which you were called, with all humility in attitude and gentleness along with long-lasting endurance, putting up with one another in love, putting out effort to maintain the unity of the spirit in the binding together of peace; *one* body and one Spirit, just as you were called in one hope of your calling, one Lord, one faith, one baptism, one God and Father of all, who is over all and through all and in all. (Eph. 4:1-6)[1]

The point this translation makes is the coordination between the unity of the Spirit and the seven ones. The unity of the Spirit is based on the reality of these seven ones. No man invented these truths, and no man's opinion will change any of them.

"Our duty is to live out a maintenance ministry on behalf of the Spirit's unity."

A closer look reveals some interesting facts about this list of seven. First, they are not all equal. The three persons of the Godhead (Father, Son, and Holy Spirit) are either originators or revealers of the other four spiritual qualities mentioned. The Godhead is the content of the other four members with a primary emphasis in the overall, through all, and in all presence of God the Father. Christ, as the Father's revelation of grace, is at the core of the entire set. The Spirit, as revealer of Christ and agent of unity, also participates in the creation of unity.

Nothing here can legitimately be used to promote division. Each point builds on the next. The one God stands squarely behind unity. Without the one body, we fragment the one Spirit. If hope has no power to weld the saved into a single unit, it is not hope.

Then, unless the one Lord is revealed as Savior by the one faith, our common needs are not met. Unless the one baptism is part of an adequate response of faith to the one Lord, it will only fragment the body and make a mockery of the Spirit's unity. Without all these elements, the one God cannot bind us all together. Nothing can be removed from this list and leave unity intact.

The Eighth One (4:7-10)

Eight ones? Yes, to the seven unifying truths, a necessary eighth is added . . . *you* . . . *me*. "But grace was given to *each of us* according to the measure of Christ's gift" (4:7). We must each accept our responsibility for the other seven to be effective.

Paul says that Christ imparts to us grace based upon his own capacity to give, and we know what is boundless (4:7). Christ gives so we may be the effective eighth factor in unity. He possesses the authority and desire to give gifts by virtue of his completed mission on earth and his return to the Father (4:8-10). Unity on a human basis is impossible, but when we reflect Christ's grace all things are possible.

A true tragedy of our time is the yearning for "gifts" to certify someone's subjective feelings about his own spiritual security. Christ's gift is for the selfless edification of the body (1 Cor. 14:12). The grace imparted to us teaches us to give so that all things Christ desires may be fulfilled (4:10). Christ graciously chooses to work through his people and equips them for his work. So Christ not only makes human oneness possible, but his generosity also makes it practical.

Foundation and Maintenance (4:13)

Christ's gifts include both the furnishing of a foundation and a maintenance ministry for the church. The apostles and prophets, gifted with the truth about Christ, provided the foundation of truth needed (2:20, 3:5). They laid the foundation and it cannot be added to or improved upon. The apostles and prophets were Christ's gift to the church so that a stable foundation might exist. All believers for all time can build upon that foundation.

The need exists in every generation to maintain this foundation. Christ's maintenance ministry helps train all saints to "maintain the unity of the Spirit in the bond of peace" (4:3). A foundation ministry and a maintenance ministry: one unique, the other a continuing need. Without regular maintenance, no structure can last.

Christ gave the maintenance ministry to the body, the church. It consists of "evangelists" and "pastor-teachers." Evangelists spread the good news about Christ. In that way faith comes, and men and women build their lives on the one foundation. Pastor-teachers (both the words in the original are governed by one article to indicate a joint function) are charged with shepherding and instructing the flock.

Evangelists and pastor-teachers must prepare God's people for useful service in the body of Christ (4:12). The maintenance ministry outfits the saints to minister and build up the body of Christ. All followers of Christ are called to serve, which is exactly what "minister" means, a servant.

We rob people when we do things for them they

should be doing for themselves. The word translated "equip" or "prepare" (4:12) is defined in the gospels as the mending of nets to make them useful or serviceable. The saints become serviceable when the maintenance ministry is doing its job. This is the church's greatest program — every member a minister.

Personal growth occurs when each member of the body moves toward the Head. The object of serving is to know the Son better and attain unity and maturity (4:13). Christianity is not some personal religious service to subscribe to like the morning paper. We do not pay our dues by attending a few services, contributing some money, and then expecting a "clergyman" to be available when we need him. Christianity is personal involvement with the Son of God. It is learning to serve with Jesus, growing up into his likeness.

Spiritual Dice-Playing (4:14)

There are too many baby Christians and too many kindergarten congregations. If the church is only a perpetual playpen for spiritual babies, how can there be service and outreach? The first priority of the maintenance ministry is to develop spiritual faculties, not physical facilities. In other words, to move the saints to maturity in Christ. *All* are expected to attain maturity, and to do it they must have knowledge of the Son of God (4:13). Christ as an ideal must be our motivation and goal.

Clever men prey on immature disciples. Like citizens greedy for quick money, they can be taken in by the devil's sly con men. Paul talks of the "cunning of men," who by "craftiness" deceive and disturb unstable believers. "Cunning" is from the Greek word *kubeia*, which comes from *Kubos*, a cube or die. *Kubeia* in Grecian times was dice-playing.

Those who disturb congregations with their clever manipulation of doctrinal opinions are dice-playing with men's souls. They whirl unstable people around like so many tops, "borne about by every wind of doctrine" (4:14).[1]

Trying to keep up with the latest doctrinal craze is like living on a turntable. Once some eager preacher students approached T.B. Larrimore, a pioneer preacher of the last century. They asked, "What stand should we take on this issue?" The old man replied, "Take no stand on that issue, take your stand on Jesus Christ." If you get the center right, the edges will come out right too.

Truthing It in Love (4:15)

How should we react to our brothers? Remember we are supposed to be ministering to them. Not as so many babies, "but being truthful in love, let us grow unto him in all things" (4:15).[1] This means honest and helpful treatment of one another. The verb here is literally "truthing it." The text includes no verb for "speaking." Dealing truly is more than speaking truly, but speaking truly is part of dealing truly. Act true — speak true, they go together.

"Truthing it" must be done completely under the influence of love for the brother. This verse is not a *carte blanche* to rebuke and tell others off with ease and dispatch. Some people delight in reading others

90

the spiritual riot act. Personal victory should not be our goal. We should want others to grow up to Christ.

"You who are spiritual," Paul says, are to undertake the "restoration" of an offender (Gal. 6:15). Only the spiritual man can have a ministry of restoration. The immature need not apply, for they will do more damage than good. When we learn to love we will know how to bring a brother back to the Lord.

Growing a Healthy Body (4:16)

The harmonious arrangement of the body is a mark of the craftsmanship of God. By calling the church a body, the apostle stresses its organic, dynamic nature. A body is interdependent. Action or inaction of any part affects all other parts. In I Corinthians 12, Paul says that each member is necessary and needed. No member is to covet or despise another's function.

The church is a body, not a gang of one-celled animals. It is not a collection of amoebas temporarily together to make a pseudo-body. A mere collection of individuals cannot share what God intended for the body. Individualism is so rampant in our world that it is difficult for us to subordinate ourselves to the interests and needs of others.

The eye does not pop out and go running off looking for a mirror in which to admire itself. The stomach, even when suffering through an attack of too much pizza, does not run off looking for a milk-drinking body. It stays around, and suffers along with the whole body. It all fits together.

Neither is the church a bag of marbles. We are not a bunch of hard-shelled atoms bumping into each other only at assemblies or so-called "fellowships." We must get out of our shells and be open to feel the pain and experience the joy of fellow members of the body.

"When each member with which the body has been supplied functions energetically it makes for the building up of the body in love (4:16)."[1] A more important lesson in church growth can hardly be found. The language of this verse does not say "when each member supplies what he has . . . ." Rather, Paul says the body has been supplied with members who must energetically (*energeo* is the word translated "working") work toward upbuilding the body in love. God has supplied each member in the body — making him available to the body by grace. When each member works as he should, growth will occur.

The type of growth discussed here does not necessarily delight a statistically-minded person. Numbers are important, of course, for they represent souls. This growth is the personal growth of those already in the body. What is the use of having people added to the body if there is no climate for further growth? Christ means for his people to grow up in love. You don't grow roses in the snow. Love is the needed environment for church growth.

Moonwalks and Balloonery

Growing up in love is Christ's ideal for his body. Any other kind of growth is malignant or, at best, balloonery. Cancers grow, but only in malignancy.

92

God wants the body to grow, not swell. If love is not constantly flowing, knitting the body together and lubricating the joints, no real growth is occurring. Even if the building where the church meets is popping at the seams, no real growth is going on if there is no love.

Every so often a street carnival comes to town. Among the attractions is a plastic bubble called a Moonwalk. Pay a quarter and bounce around like a rubber ball for fifteen minutes. A small motor drives a steady stream of hot air into the bubble to keep it inflated. At the end of the day, the operator shuts the motor down and pulls the plug on the bubble. All that's left of the Moonwalk is a wad of shriveled plastic. The church is not to be that way. It is to be built up in love, not puffed up by hot air. Edification, not inflation, is our need.

The church at Ephesus must not have heeded Paul's instructions about building the body up in love. Later they received another letter directly from Jesus Christ. The letter states: "I have against you that you do not love as you did at first" (Rev. 2:4). They were warned that loss of love means loss of life: "I will remove your lampstand . . ." (Rev. 2:5).

We will lose our place with Jesus if we do not continue to build in love toward Christ. Our Lord says a church without love does not deserve to exist.

We had better listen.

Futility 8

Sometimes we wonder why a Christian, a person delivered from the sinfulness of his old life, still has such a struggle against evil. The New Testament does not teach absolute sinlessness of the child of God. John 1:8-9 states this clearly:

> If we say we have no sin, we are deceiving ourselves and the truth is not in us. If we will admit our sins, he is to be trusted and he is just to forgive our sins and clean us from all wrong-doing.[1]

Even in his new life, a Christian still struggles against sin. But he has changed sides in the battle. In the old life he was a prisoner of the forces of evil. He had no power to do what was right. But God's Son conducted a raid on the enemy and freed us from his camp. After our rescue Christ did not put us in the rear so we would forget a war was going on. Instead, he placed us on the front line in the battle against evil. Now we are on the winning side. Now we have a

Commander-in-Chief with power to defeat the enemy. The struggle goes on, but in Christ victory is assured.

The old life still seems to have attractions. Sometimes we may grow weary of the struggle and long for the peace and quiet of being prisoners again. We are like the wilderness wanderers, who longed to be back in Egypt again where they were in bondage. That's when we need to take a long look at the way it was. Think of the kind of "walk" we had in the old life, and the creative struggle of the new "walk" will again be vindicated.

Sharing Delusions (4:17)

Paul uses the ethical term "walk" again, this time with an emphatic negative (4:17, KJV). Some ways of life are not productive, even though they seem to be attractive. The old life had its apparent attractions, as it does for many today. The biggest draw comes from the sheer desire to conform. Humans have a tenacious tendency to conform. How difficult it is to resist what is going on all around you. The believer will probably seem out of step with the world, strangely different (1 Pet. 4:4).

The pull of the old life will be even stronger when we are thrown into company with those still in the devil's camp. The camp has no physical walls, and the prisoners think they are really free. They talk about their freedom and their lack of inhibitions. They share their delusions with others, even those born again. For this reason Paul wants the believer to completely abandon the old territory. Don't look back — remember Lot's wife!

Paul strongly reinforces his warning by solemnly appealing to his authority "in the Lord" (4:17). The Lord does not want his people to conform to anybody's morality or conduct except His. He especially does not want them to act as their culture has taught them. They should be able to see, from their new perspective, how the evil in their former lives was a result of bad thinking, of an empty mind. "The futility of their minds" is the source of this world's misdirected lives (4:17).

The word translated "futility" means a state of emptiness, nonproductivity, or purposelessness. The proud culture of the Gentile world was really empty because it lacked spiritual depth and purpose. What good were the magnificent achievements of the Greeks? What purpose was achieved by those who mastered the intricacies of architecture, mathematics, and philosophy? Though we catch a glimpse of moral light in a Socrates or Plato, though we thrill to the eloquence of a Demosthenes and admire the poems of a Pindar, still we look in vain for spiritual insight and fulfillment.

Travelers to Nashville, Tennessee, marvel as they examine the replica of the Parthenon built there. It is inspiring to stand on those massive steps and look up at the beautifully-proportioned pillars. But despite all this glorious grandeur, the culture was empty where it counted most. Without lives directed by God all earthly accomplishments turn to dust. Man without God is hollow. No development of the soul means what is greatest and most glorious of all has eluded us.

A Futile Faith (4:18)

Our modern culture is also purposeless apart from God. We have added one dimension, though, which many pagans also had: a faith of sorts. Secular man must have an idealogy to support his world-view, so he chooses a secular faith. But this is also empty. He believes in such things as the inevitable progress of man and the relativity of all things. Even his faith is empty.

"Futility" comes because of perceptual limitations. These people leave no room in their lives for God, therefore they are doomed to a walk of vanity and purposelessness. Academically and technologically, modern man is a giant. Spiritually, he is a pygmy.

Paul has established that the pagan life is fruitless and purposeless. "But it looks like such fun," someone sighs. The person who desires to be one of the "beautiful people" or to swing with the jet set shows the same empty-headedness Paul warns against. Such distorted views of happiness are riding a moral elevator with only a *down* button.

Down, down the pagan moral consciousness descends. Paul tracks its course: "Darkened as far as their understanding goes" (4:18).[1] No light shines at such depths. Here there is perpetual mental twilight. If there, light would only show what was really happening to people pursuing their aimless ends of fun and happiness. Light would reveal the moral cancer eating at their souls. But they want no light: "They hate the light for their deeds are evil" (John 3:20).[1] They have no real intellectual arguments

97

against the light, yet they use bogus logic to keep the light at a distance.

"When a man is blind to true values, true joy, the true life, true freedom, and true insights, he is an ignorant person."

They are "strangers" to (*alienated from*, KJV) the life of God"(4:18). There is a different basis for life, a different source of life, the life of God. It is life indeed. Real life, though, is an alien experience to an empty man or woman. The healthy life of God seems abnormal to them. The sickest patients can sometimes convince themselves that their condition is normal. So the moral life has its "sickness unto death" where all that is "good and true" seems a threat to "freedom and fun." When such people tear up the good, stable foundations of home and society, they think they are tearing down a dungeon. They are actually destroying their own houses. Soon there will be no place to go.

What's the problem? Ignorance (4:18). Ignorance creates a moral callus around the heart. Tell a modern hedonist that he thinks like he does because he is ignorant, and he's apt to reply: "Me? Ignorant? Why I'm enlightened. It's you religious people that are ignorant." A man may have more degrees than a thermometer, yet be ignorant in vital areas. When a man is blind to true values, true joy, the true life, true freedom, and true insights, he is an ignorant person.

Paul is not talking about the kind of ignorance in people with little knowledge. The pagans were not uneducated, except on the subject of God. Yet it was this one area of ignorance that was fatal. So it is today. Some very erudite persons can be ignorant about some things that matter most.

Just a few decades after the spread of Christianity into the remote corners of the Roman Empire, a noted pagan writer named Lucian encountered disciples of Jesus. Lucian, an educated man, a poet, a man of letters, a worldy-wise satirist, revealed his true ignorance of what matters most when he wrote:

> The poor wretches (Christians) have convinced themselves, first and foremost, that they are going to be immortal and live for all time, in consequence of which they despise death and willingly give themselves into custody, most of them. Furthermore, their first Lawgiver persuaded them that they are all brothers of one another after they have transgressed once for all by denying the Greek gods and by worshipping that crucified sophist himself and living under his laws. (Lucian, *The Passing of Peregrinus*.)

This reflects on Lucian, not Christ. How did Lucian feel about death and his fellowman? His ignorance blocked the way.

Expert Ignorance

An expert speaking out of his field is also ignorant. In the academic world, occasionally a professor will take a passing swipe at the Bible or Christianity. He would never think of rendering an academic judgment in a field he had not studied, but he thinks nothing of commenting on the Christian faith. No scholar in the field of English would dare comment on the theory of subatomic particles, but it's free game on religious matters.

Just because a man may be an expert on John Milton or alpha waves does not mean he knows anything about the faith. When he spends as much time on the Bible and living for Jesus as he has on academic work, then we can listen with a bit of respect.

The trouble is, as someone has said, "We're all ignorant, just on different subjects." Spiritual ignorance is the worst sort of ignorance, especially when so much is at stake. It isn't as if there is no spiritual information around. There is no excuse (Rom. 1:20).

The Lord's own people dare not fall back into ignorance either. We must be careful not to deify ignorance and take an anti-intellectual stance. The Bible says the followers of Christ are disciples, which means students or learners. The Lord does not want his people to be ignorant. One day, so a story goes, a preacher was extolling the virtues of his ignorance: "Thank God I'm an ignorant man," he hollered. "In fact, I pray to God that he will make me even more ignorant." At which point a listener said to his neighbor "That is the most impossible request I have ever heard."

The Moral Elevator (4:19)

The Lord can use an ignorant man, but he cannot use his ignorance. Ignorance of what counts most is a pagan attitude. Remaining in ignorance is the surest way to stay on the downward trip. The basement stop on the moral elevator is the loss of all sensitivity. All feeling and sensitivity gone! Last stop! To become insensitive to evil and wrongdoing is the ultimate trip into nonhuman status (4:19). People like this can be amazingly sensitive to financial or other matters of material concern, but totally insensitive to what has transcending value.

About the same time as this epistle, a writer of satire named Petronius wrote about an incident at a banquet he attended. Petronius had been invited to the house of Trimalchio, a self-important ex-slave. In the middle of the feast a servant appeared and began reading loudly from Trimalchio's business ledger:

> Born on July 26 on Trimalchio's estate at Cumae, thirty male and forty female slaves.
> Item, 500,000 bushels of wheat transferred from the threshing rooms into storage.
> On the same date, the slave Mithridates crucified alive for blaspheming the guardian spirit of our master Gaius.
> On the same date, the sum of 300,000 returned to the safe because it could not be invested.
> On the same date, in the gardens of Pompeii, fire broke out in the house of the bailiff Nasta.
> "What?" roared Trimalchio. "When did I buy any gardens at Pompeii?"

Trimalchio was not alone in his insensitivity to what was truly valuable (bailiff Nasta's safety or the slave's cruel death). Is our world much different?

"Being past feeling" (4:19)[1] means being morally insensitive. Truth and morals always suffer when men get this insensitive to spiritual reality. Wantonness and uncleanliness result from this hardening of the spiritual arteries. Wantonness (Greek *aselgeia*) is a boastful and arrogant display of what is wrong as if it was normal behavior. Things are really turned upside down when this bold sinning is prevalent.

In Germany during World War II a birthday party was given for von Ribbentrop, the foreign minister. As Albert Speer reports it, the Foreign Minister was given a copy of every treaty he had negotiated which Germany had broken. Everyone considered it a good joke. Even Hitler had a little laugh at this indecent parody on international honesty. If the handwriting on the wall ever appeared to such insensitive, wanton people, they would criticize the penmanship! Yet the handwriting is there.

"Futility comes because of profound perceptual limitations."

God will expect an answer to this horrible mutilation of man's spiritual nature. Man stifles the truth at his own peril. Yet, such insensitivity does not satisfy immoral people. The more they get, the more they want. Lust is a bottomless pit. What they have is never enough.

Being morally desensitized leads to further surrender: "They have surrendered themselves to wantonness which results in the practice of all that is unclean with an insatiable lust for more" (4:19).[1] The unending desire for more governs this wanton surrender. Pornography merchants say it is difficult to maintain an audience unless they keep finding greater depths of depravity to show them. Unclean actions only create an unending search for more thrills. Evil men are greedy for something that has no power to satisfy. Their life cannot satisfy them because it has no goal larger than their self-pleasure. Their pursuit of self-pleasure only leads to more boredom. Jesus knew the source of real satisfaction: "Blessed are those who hunger and thirst for righteousness, for they shall be satisfied" (Matt. 5:6).

The word *pleonexia*, the heart of the old life, is usually translated as "greediness" or "covetousness." But its more literal meaning, "a desire for more," seems appropriate here. All their unclean works are done in a vain sphere of nonsatisfaction. The old life is like a dog chasing his tail.

A New Life (4:20-24)

The old life needs to be thrust away (4:22). It is going nowhere fast. Like a runaway train off its track, a crackup is inevitable. Someone must lay a hand on the controls in a hurry. That someone is available. He is Jesus.

Ephesians 4:20 contains a marvelous insight: "You did not learn Christ this way."[1] They had been taught that direction for their new life came from Christ. Christ had not saved them initially, then left them to live the new life by their own guidelines and

103

impulses. Christ is the head — Lord — of the new life also. Christ provides the direction for moral living as well as initial salvation.

Christ does not lead backward, but forward. Forward into moral progress and growth in the image of Christ. There is no excuse for a Christian to stand still morally. He may stay in the same job, but he cannot stay in the same frame of mind after his conversion (4:23).

Paul says the truth about moral living is in Jesus (4:21). The call to Christian morality is not an appeal to a list of rules, but an appeal for people to base morality on the life and actions of Jesus. The truth is "in Jesus!" Peter makes the same appeal when he says to "arm yourselves with the attitude"[1] of Christ (1 Pet. 4:1). The follower of Christ does not follow a list of rules, but he follows the life of Christ. We are called to be like him, and this calls for an authentic morality. To live like Jesus is to live as true a life as possible.

Putting Off the Old

Christian morality, then, is based on the character of God. When we see that God is the most important factor in our lives, we will treat ourselves and others in a moral way. He who "loves the Lord our God" will have no trouble "loving his neighbor like himself." The truth in Jesus helps a man or woman see the old life as it really is — futile.

The word "put off" means to thrust away if a person has something clinging to him (4:22). We would say, "Get rid of it." Because of the truth in Jesus we are able to get rid of the old life. Maximus

Tyrius, a writer of the second century A.D., used this verb in an interesting way. He said, "Thrust away the role of spectator and become a contestant." There appears an element of renunciation in the word. We are to get rid of, by renouncing, the old way of life.

We renounce the old life by the power of the truth in Jesus. At last we see it for what it is, a corrupt and deceitful parody of human existence. However, we should not stand around admiring our decision to forsake the old life. We should clean out the demons and open the door to a new tenant. Jesus is to settle in (4:23-24). He will renew our minds, clothing us with the new man (4:23-23).

Putting on the New (4:23-24)

Our minds need renewing so that we may see things from the new point of view. The old way of life clouded our mind and understanding (4:17-19). Now, at last, we can see clearly. A fresh breeze from God has blown away the immoral smog. We must keep this fresh outlook and perspective, or the mists of the old life will close in on us again.

When our daughters were small they enjoyed "dressing up" in their mother's clothing. The clothing made them feel grown up. Paul talks about a new wardrobe for people with a new outlook. This wardrobe is not a costume for a game of charades, but a completely new person. Our empty hearts will be filled with the most important Guest. The old rags of our sinfulness have been replaced by more appropriate clothing to entertain this Guest.

105

Our new mind requires a new man to go with it. The new man is God's creation (Eph. 2:10). As the first man was created by God, so the new man is created by God. The new man is created by God to live in righteousness and truthful holiness. God did not make the new man to look longingly back on the futility of his old life. The new man is now oriented toward new attitudes and actions. At last he is on his way up.

Imitators 9

Everybody has a birthday. Christians have two birthdays though, one on the day of their natural birth and the other on the day of their spiritual birth. On the first we become a person, on the second a new person (4:24). To remain a new person, we must continue "putting off" negative attitudes and actions (4:25ff).[1] Fortunately we have a great model to follow in attaining our new personhood. Our God, who is now our Father, calls upon his children to imitate his life and character (5:1), but we are not copycats. It is an honor to have such a great model to follow.

In an age of cheap fads and plastic imitations, God calls us to pattern ourselves after what is real! Our salvation is not a do-it-yourself proposition. Many men can hardly wait for a night or a weekend so they may play "do-it-yourself" in the garage. Christianity is not that way. Even though we imitate Jesus, it is still He who saves. Jesus did not drag us across the line of initial salvation, then say "I've brought you this far, now you do the rest yourself." Jesus not only rescues us from the old life, he is also the Lord of the new life.

Paul makes this point very clearly in Romans (5:1ff). Jesus died for us when we were sinners, ungodly, alienated from God. But, and this is most emphatic, now that we are saved by Jesus' death, we continue to be saved by his life:

> Much more, then, especially since we have now been justified by his blood shall we be saved from wrath through him. For if while we were enemies we were reconciled to God through the death of his son, much more, since we are now reconciled shall we be saved by his life.[1] (Rom. 5:9-10)

Paul clearly indicates the saving life of Jesus is the dynamic power for the Christian's new life.

Because we now live for God, we have a new motivation to creative living. Because the Father cares, we can live meaningful lives that make a difference. The futility of wasted living is in the pagan past. The future stretches before us as one creative opportunity after another. No longer will we make life up as we go along. We realize, as someone has said, "Life is what's happening to you while you're making other plans." The creative imitation Paul moves toward involves us in the meaningful life of God (5:1).

In Jesus we find not only the will but the power to live the new life. The culture of Paul's day rejected life as a creative experience. The world of his time lost its nerve! Life seemed to be going nowhere, and apart from God it was.

Petronius of Rome recorded an encounter one of his contemporaries had with the Sybil at Cumae in the first century A.D. The Sybil was a female oracle, a kind of fortune-teller. The inquirer asked her (because it is so touching, we preserve the question and answer in the original Greek with a translation added):

Sibulla ti theleis? =Sybil, what is it you wish?
Apothanein thelo =I wish to die.

Even one supposedly possessed of supernatural powers had no desire to go on in a meaningless life. How different it is for the follower of Jesus who everyday discovers the "day the Lord has made." How fresh and clean the new life is amidst the other decaying, purposeless lives in our world.

New Life Directions (4:25-27)

How should a Christian oppose the corrosive tendencies of the old life? By adopting a new code of legalism? No. If legalism could not save in the first place, it's no use bringing it in the back door. We oppose the old life by replacing it with the expansive power of new life. New growth demands new roots.

The new life, however, does require consistent and conscious decisions to follow certain actions and shun others. Behavior which is unacceptable to the partaker of new life is to be "thrust away." Paul warns his hearers to be hungry for the source of right actions. We are to thrust away "the lie" (4:25)[1] because "we are members one of another."

Anger is not to be protracted (4:26). A continued grudge delivers you to the devil. Such hostility gives

109

the devil an opportunity to subvert the new life (4:27). Replace anger with a forgiving attitude.

The new life directions are rooted in a fertile seedbed of insights into the nature of the new person (4:25-5:5). The new man is concerned about what effect his actions have on others. He does not lie because lies destroy the integrity of relationships (4:25). The new life cannot survive and grow without honesty and openness. Lies deliver people over to false relationships. A person who deceives others also deceives himself. The new life and deceitfulness are not compatible. No relationship can survive the continued practice of falsification.

The new man cannot afford to let his anger run riotously onward. The new life possesses a gentleness toward others that is destroyed by perpetual temper indulgences. Paul recognizes that we will be angry on occasions. Some things ought to make us angry. But to be mastered by anger lets our growing soul leak out through the holes in our temperament.

No one can love God while hating another human being (1 John 4:20). If anger arises in our souls, find out its cause. Is it because we have been put on the defensive by someone? Are we insecure? Whatever we do don't let it protract our anger. Tell it to be out of town by sundown.

The Controlled Life

Paul is really telling us that the new life is the controlled life. The last of the fruit-cluster of the Spirit is self-control (Gal. 5:23). "The spirit of the prophets is controlled by the prophets" (1 Cor. 14:32).[1]

We have so deified spontaneous reactions in our culture that we think control and planning are stifling. We even plan to have spontaneity. Some people think anything that is thought-out is worthless. The impulse of the moment, that's the thing! We have already seen that God does not think this way (1:3-14). God planned our salvation before the world was founded. Fervency and control are not enemies.

There can be no real ardor without order. Control and mastery are elements of God's character. The new life features a control of self developed by the Spirit. Unchecked anger and violence are not expressions of the new life, but the old.

We live in such a violent world that it is easy for us to see anger as a virtue. C. Vann Woodward details in *The New South* that after the Civil War the southern United States was one of the bloodiest, most violent sections in the entire world. Our romantic dreams of moonlight and magnolia dissolve in the reality of human anger and brutality. Only God can tame such a destructive spirit. The new man learns that protracted anger gives the devil his opportunity (4:27). When we lack control over our temper, it means the devil controls our lives.

Replacing Evil

The new person learns to replace what is evil and destructive with what is good and constructive. We learn to let what we stand *for* drive out what we

111

should stand against. It is practical to replace bad attitudes and actions with good.

An overweight person on a diet usually does better if he doesn't go around saying, "Don't eat fats, don't eat sweets, don't eat this, don't eat that." If, instead, he eats wholesome, nonfattening food, he finds he has no appetite for food he should avoid. He replaced the hunger which would have ruined his diet. There is no power in reciting only the things we are against. We drive out the opportunity for wrongdoing by actually practicing good things. Soon then we drive out both temptation and impulse and develop a taste for what is good. We are moving forward in our imitation of God's life.

Work What Is Good (4:28)

The case of the thief illustrates this principle (4:28). The person saved from a lifetime of stealing is not merely told to stop stealing. He is encouraged to work honestly and share the fruit of his labor with needy people. He is given an opportunity to serve others, not the devil. He becomes creative. He contributes to the good. He replaces bad and destructive habits with habits that help him and others.

Stealing is a major problem in our society. Muggers and thieves are so active in some cities that people cringe in fear behind their locked doors. Better laws and courts may help a little, but the heart of the world must be changed. Sometimes, sadly, even Christians engage in petty (and sometimes not so petty) thievery, then wonder why their moral example is so poorly appreciated by a watching world.

A man, supposedly a believer in Christ, complained loudly about the dishonesty in the schools. "Some lousy punk stole a bunch of pencils from my kid at school," he moaned. "I don't know what kids are coming to today, they're so dishonest. Of course, I can get all the pencils I want from the storeroom down at the office, but it's the principle of the thing." Parson Weems is supposed to have added to his biography of Washington the fable about young George chopping down the cherry tree. He wanted to teach honesty to young people. He forgot to mention it was a fable!

"To imitate meant . . . not mere impersonation, but receiving inspiration from a good model."

A former thief should use his hands to work for what is good (4:28). He now produces good work. Paul says what is accomplished by a person's occupation is good. That is, he does a good job. Sometimes zealous Christians think earning a living imposes on the time they could be spending working for the Lord. When a person is doing a good job he is working for the Lord!

Believers who cluster around a water cooler are wrong if they think a poor day's work can be redeemed by saying a word for Christ, or handing out tracts to nonbelievers. The quality of the Christian's work probably speaks more eloquently

113

of what he thinks of the Lord than any tract could. A shoddy work performance reflects on the Lord. When a Christian learns a job, occupation, or profession, he should learn to do a good job. He should study hard and apply himself so when someone comes to him for help he can do a competent job. Anything less reflects discredit on the Lord.

No patient would like to hear a brain surgeon say, "I'm a little worried about this surgery. While the class was studying this I was having a religious discussion." Applying yourself *is* a Christian concern!

If we are alert the Lord will give us opportunities to work and study with nonbelievers. Our profession of the faith will have a solid, practical demonstration if we consistently do a good job at our work. This is an excellent recommendation of the new life in action.

Decaying Words (4:29)

Sins of the tongue are among the most irritating and destructive. Paul speaks of these vocal abberations as "rotten" (4:29).[1] The word *sapros* suggests what is decayed, like our word *saprophyte* which refers to a fungus existing on decayed matter. Foul speech is rotten, useless for any positive purpose. And Paul expands on tongue sins in Ephesians 5:4. We are to avoid "shameful talk,"[1] which means "ugly talk."

Thoughtless sins of the tongue are not appropriate for God's people. They should concentrate on constructive behavior, not destructive (4:29).

Humor or wit are not banned, for Bible writers frequently use these forms of speech. Jesus' portrayal of the man wrestling to extract a speck from his brother's eye, while he has a large board protruding from his own, contains rare and thoughtful humor.

The apostle addresses himself to the thoughtless and profitless ridicule of others, as well as the use of crude, disgusting, and lewd words. Those in the new life must firmly resist and reject such actions. The tongue is used to upbuild and give grace to listeners. Of all the sins for which restitution can never adequately be made, sins of the tongue must lead the list. Like murder, vicious words leave their victims prostrate in the dust. The attitudes of verse 32 will put the mouth menace to a well-deserved death.

Frustrating the Spirit (4:30)

Failing to change our attitudes frustrates what the Spirit of God is trying to do in our new life. Paul speaks of this as "making the Spirit sorry" (4:30).[1] The verb form suggests this possible translation: "Stop grieving the Holy Spirit . . . " This happens when the Christian fails to alter some basic attitudes (4:31).

When we are resentful and bitter, angry and big-mouthed, the Holy Spirit is frustrated from developing the fruit of the Spirit in our lives. Arndt-Gingrich suggest that an alternate translation for the verb "grieve" would be "irritate." "Stop irritating the Holy Spirit" would then be the thrust of the imperative statement. We inhibit spiritual

115

progress and irritate the Spirit when we tenaciously hold on to attitudes typical of pagan people.

Imitators of God (5:1)

We do not usually think of imitations as being desirable. Imitation diamonds or pearls are not valued like the real thing. But there is a place for some genuine imitation: imitating God. The word translated "imitators" was more meaningful to people in the ancient world than to us (5:1).

Ancient rhetorical theory included a concept called *mimesis,* or imitation. It meant, in the best ancient thought, not mere impersonation, but receiving inspiration from a good model. The good model inspired the student to reach for the excellence displayed by the prototype.

The context indicates a simpler but similar idea may be predominant. The believer is to imitate his Father as a "beloved child" (5:1). Children who are loved want to be like their parents. Remember you are a child who is deeply loved by your heavenly Father. Realizing this causes us to want to be like our Father. We want to model ourselves on his characteristics, attitudes, and actions. This is positive imitation.

Positive imitation is creative, while negative imitation is thoughtless and faddish. What is popularly called "doing your own thing" is the most slavish sort of artificial, inferior behavior. Following the model of God avoids crushing conformity. We should act because we are loved, and because we love the Lover. We'll never find a better model than God.

116

Walking in Love (5:2-4)

It is natural that beloved children "walk in love" (5:2). Paul insists on the ethical term "walk." Love is not abstract or just a feeling. Love acts. It is the environment of our walk. Love every step of the way is his message. The new life teaches the believer to move from the stance of "falling in love" to the position of "being in love."

People today love to fall in love. They are not too excited about staying in love. Yet staying in love is exactly the walk of the new life. Falling in love is romanticized in a thousand moon-June songs, but hardly any celebrate staying in love. Romantics like the idea of falling in love. They love to look for starlight, moonlight, and firecrackers going off in their hearts. Staying in love is not so spectacular. It takes hard work, dedication, and endurance. Yet, at some point, if love is ever to grow, falling in love must become staying in love.

To stay in love requires the discovery and building upon more stable characteristics than first attracted you to the person. At first you may have been attracted by appearance, the outward mannerisms, and the qualities you thought you saw. For the relationship to become "staying in love," you must find more stable realities such as loyalty, reliability, gentleness, and communication. If you lack these qualities or refuse to develop them it will be difficult to stay in love. But if you build the relationship on these more stable qualities, staying in love will be better than falling in love.

In religious matters people also like to fall in love, but find it hard to stay in love. They want the skyrockets and mental quivers that go with falling in love. They want their religion to be the moon-June sort all the time. Certainly entering a relationship with the God of heaven is exciting, but we should not think of it like a romantic daydream. Our love for God should be a "staying in love" type of love. Our relationship is with God's steadfast love, faithfulness, generous forgiveness, and desire to better us.

Staying in Love (5:5)

Walking in love means staying in love with God. Love is not primarily a matter of emotions, but a matter of the will. Our will has been freely yielded to God, and we feel good emotionally because God demonstrated love for us.

Emotional feeling has a place in Christianity, for our emotions are part of our total being. But we are not controlled by the emotional part of our love. We feel good because we know God loves us and we are walking in love toward him and our fellow man. These are objective facts, and feeling always should follow fact. We feel good about our physical health when we know the doctor has examined us and established the fact that we are healthy.

You cannot love God and the world at the same time (James 4:4). Our inheritance is secure as long as we continue to depend on Christ and walk in love (5:5). We surrender all that is truly valuable when we lapse back into pagan morality. Such behavior is symptomatic of falling under the sway of a lesser love, being overpowered by a malignant influence.

A married man I know realized he had a great wife. She had all the attributes to make him truly happy, but he came under the power of another woman. She did not have his best interests at heart and would gladly wreck his home for her own pleasure. He was too imperceptive to see that this "love" was destroying his only real love. The fatal attraction of the world is illusive and invariably destructive.

No greater love than God's exists. The new life is a call to "walk in love." The highest tribute we can bring to our Father is imitating him by walking in love.

A higher love has called imitators of God away from copycat conformity to the world. In the next section the apostle will show them another marvelous truth: Christians are not only children of love, but also children of light.

Light 10

Light does amazing things. It moves faster than anything else we know of. It can also heal, kill, communicate, and illuminate. Light is versatile and indispensable.

Paul focuses on light in this section. Light turns out to be as indispensable in the moral realm as in the physical. It keeps us from being deceived about some important matters.

"Let no one deceive you with empty words . . ." (5:6). After an extended discussion of sins of the tongue, the believer should recognize the mouth menace. The persuasion the unbeliever employs, though, is likely to be so subtle in its promises that even triple warnings are not enough. Paul encourages the disciple to look behind the rhetoric to the substance of what is being said. Behind these glossy appeals is barren sterility.

The multitude of soft sex, fashion, and romance magazines may present a slick "with-it" appearance.

They may tell you they are doing their bit to free you of your inhibitions. Madison Avenue may try to convince you that a certain brand of booze will make you dynamic and dashing. A seemingly sincere friend may counsel that you're taking your religion too seriously. You need to relax and have a "little fun." All very persuasive, and all dead wrong! Invitations to emptiness and futility. That's how it was and is. Remember? (4:17ff).

There are too many talkers who haven't considered the consequences of their recommendations. Ancient Greeks had a comic word for a noisy talker. He was a *lalobaruparamelorythmobates*. This mouthful referred to the nonsense nature of what he was recommending. Remember that the next time you hear some persuasive emptiness. The speaker might be a *lalobaruparamelorythmobates*!

The Terror of Darkness (5:7-8)

Persuasion has been raised nearly to the status of a science. Some pseudo-religious movements employ coercive persuasion (brainwashing). But we can resist this threat if we remember that we are "children of light" (5:8)

Light has a wonderful way of exposing dark corners. A flood of illumination from the Lord's word will reveal the true nature of what sounded so plausible. This, plus our realization that God is deadly serious in his opposition to sin, moves us to stay in the light (5:7).

Light is our abode as Christians. We need it to grow and live. A kind of spiritual photosynthesis goes on in the Christian's life when he is exposed to God's light. You can't raise sunflowers in the basement. Believers are called to be sonflowers — illumined in their total beings by the Son of God.

"Light, by a kind of spiritual photosynthesis, produces enlightened persons who demonstrate their parentage by goodness, righteousness, and truth."

People in the moral basement where the light is dim enjoy company. So Paul warns: "Don't, then, become partners with them" (5:7).[1] And why not? "Because you were at one time darkness, but now you are light in the Lord" (5:8).[1] Paul does not say we were "in the dark," but that we "were darkness." Darkness and the sinner are the same.

C.S. Lewis, the late English scholar, marveled at John's perceptiveness when Judas departed from the Lord's table (John 13:30).[1] "Judas went out, and it was night." This is more than just a report on the time of day. Darkness was not only the environment of the sinner, it was his heart.

"Now you are light in the Lord; walk as children of light" (5:8). The Lord has altered our basic nature. Darkness has been banished and light has come flooding into our lives. At first we see dimly, but as we go on with the Lord, his light allows us to see clearer and clearer what our walk is to be. "In thy light do we see light" (Ps. 36:9).

Light was one of the most powerful images in the ancient world. Nights were inky dark then. We have so much artificial light today we have lost the terror of darkness that permeated the ancient world. Ancient people who dared to venture out at night could barely see by holding a flickering torch. Grotesque shadows danced menacingly around them. Daylight was treasured. A man felt safe then. He could work. He was secure.

To say that Christians are "light in the Lord" suggests that you can feel secure with them. They will banish the shadows of evil and fear. Christians are in league with what is productive and trustworthy. Where men are under the influence of Christ, there is light.

Children of Light (5:9-10)

The church is called to be the "light of the world" (Matt. 5:14). Of course, Christ is the real light of the world and we reflect his glorious light. Still, we should not be a mushroom hidden in an obscure corner. We are to be visible. Even if we have to meet in caves and catacombs, we are to shine with a moral and spiritual brightness that will show men the way to the Lord.

We are "children of light," and the fact that light can have children shows that light is productive (5:9). Light, by a kind of spiritual photosynthesis, produces enlightened persons who demonstrate their parentage by goodness, righteousness, and truth. An enlightened person, in the New Testament, was not just "bright" intellectually. He was not just intellectually productive, but ethically and spiritually productive.

There is no separation between mental and physical service in the life of the person serving God. Man is to serve God with all his being (Luke 10:27). The brainy Christian may believe his only calling is thinking and debating. He may devour tomes by the ton, yet be in the dark by not involving himself in personal outreach. Paul says the child of light is one who does good. Thinking right and doing right go together toward pleasing the Lord (5:10).

Keep the Lights On (5:11)

Only light can show the true nature of darkness. "And do not engage in any fellow-sharing with the unfruitful works of darkness, but you should rather reprove them" (5:11).[1] After being enlightened and seeing the reality of evil, we should not want to be in the dark again.

Turning out the lights will not make what the light has revealed go away. In Louisiana, where our family lived for nearly seven years, we had trouble keeping large water bugs out of the house. We weren't lazy, we were clean, we sprayed. It's just that in South Louisiana these large roaches live outside and at night they sneak into your house to forage for goodies. You might enter your kitchen late at night with the lights off and think everything was nice and clean. One flip of the switch, though, revealed the presence of unwanted visitors. Turning off the lights did not make them go away, it just invited more in! The only way to get rid of them was to turn the lights on and go after them.

A lot of people think turning off the light of Christ in their lives makes everything all right. Actually, the true condition is otherwise — many unwanted denizens of the darkness sneak in.

"Don't share in the unfruitful works of darkness" (5:11).[1] We forsake the clean air above ground and go to live in some cave when we move backward into sharing with such unproductive darkness-dwellers. It's like becoming a moral mole and thinking the darkness of our tunnel is a normal condition. Believers have been changed and adapted for a life in the sunshine of God's love.

Eagles or Bats? (5:12-13)

How could we go back underground where people do things which are too shameful to be spoken of (5:12)? We're not made to live in the dark. That would be like an eagle soaring in the bright sky above mountaintops, suddenly taking on the behavior of a bat.

"All things reproved by the light are made evident, for all that is made evident is light" (5:13).[1] Light shows what needs to be reproved. Reproving means critically examining something to see what it really is. In ancient times, it meant to examine an issue to expose its true nature. This true exposure by the light helps us evaluate and deal objectively with what we have encountered. The searching rays of light show the clear outline in relief. This serene clarity penetrates the outward attractiveness and exposes the underlying reality. It's a moral X-ray.

Seeing the true condition of things renews our commitment to the Lord of light, Jesus Christ. We awake to the abnormal conditions of living apart from the light. Accepting this reproof means a return to normal vision. We know living underground is never normal for a believer. We realize our conversion was a call to live so that light is our normal habitat.

Making the Most of Light (5:14-16)

The call to conversion is a call to live in the light forever. Paul apparently quotes part of an early hymn (5:14). F.F. Bruce believes it is a chant sung at a prospective convert's baptism. The lines in the original (5:14) are a metrical triplet, which indicates such an explanation is probably true. What a beautiful sight it must have been to see a group of believers circle a pagan coming to faith in Christ. As he stood in the baptismal water, the group sang to him:

> *Egeire, ho katheudon*
> *kai anasta ek ton nekron,*
> *kai epiphausei soi ho Christos*

Rise, You who sleep
   and be raised from the dead,
and upon you will shine the Christ.

In a moment he was "light in the Lord."[1]

"Watch out, then, how you walk, not as unwise, but as wise, buying out opportunities for the days are evil" (5:15-16).[1] Children of light, Paul affirms, are not children in understanding. Seeing clearly, they still can see through. The disciple of the Lord is aware of his surroundings. He is not so heavenly that he is no earthly good.

Thomas More, lord chancellor of England in Henry VIII's reign, when told Henry was furious with More's opposition to the royal divorce, replied: "I know the map of England as well as any man." He knew what was going on. We should know the map of the world, not necessarily to travel it, but to spot the location of its pitfalls.

We are to be wise, not ignorant. If ignorance were a virtue, some people would be most virtuous. The Lord's servant, though, is alert to opportunities, not smugly content in ignorant apathy. The Lord sends opportunities, and to waste them is to throw away what may not be regained. We must use the opportunity while it is there, but we must first recognize it.

What good is having a light if you're not going to use it? We must not be so busy manning the fort that we fail to use our offensive opportunities to take lost ground back from the devil. The greatest sin can be just "holding our own." Wasted opportunities are lost opportunities. Enlightened people reach out.

The enlightened Christian stands above the world-citizen, who spends his time trying to forget that he is *spending* his time. The Christian uses time wisely, the worldly person tries to make it go by as fast as he can. One is alert, the other would like to become as fuzzy as possible. Among the latter are those who spend their days anesthetizing themselves with alcohol or drugs (5:18). Paul says this behavior is *asotia*, which means dissipation or waste. The prodigal son in Luke 15 lived this way ("he wasted his substance . . ."). Dissipation here is squandering what is valuable, our lives.

The nonbeliever wastes his life. A Christian who wastes his precious time and opportunities in senseless activities completely reverses the productive effects of light. To turn to drinking or some other form of chemical in-filling is sheer waste. The person who drinks or is numb on prescription drugs is probably trying to fill a wasted emptiness, but he only expands the vast wasteland of his life. No problem can be solved by a solution which is a greater problem itself. Only Christ can furnish what the empty man needs.

Under the Influence (5:18)

"Be filled with the Spirit" (5:18). All people are filling themselves with something. Some with alcohol and drugs, some with delusions of their own greatness. Some with visions of worldly power, ambition, or success. Some with the numbing effects of a hedonistic sensualism.

There is an alternative. Paul calls upon the disciple of the Lord to "be filled with the Spirit." Christ provides a way for us to be filled with what is good and productive, not wasteful. Men and women, even Christians, fill themselves with things which have no power to satisfy. We need to have a "garage sale of the soul" and clear out all the junk that takes up space and doesn't add value.

If we drink to eliminate our inferior feelings, Christ can help us love ourselves. If we drink to be socially acceptable, Christ will give us people who will not demand such personal wastefulness. If we drink to get rid of our inhibitions, Christ will free us from limitations so we may serve with confidence. If we drink to forget the pain of living, Christ can make us so alive that living will again be a great joy. Fill yourselves with what is good and the bad will not find a place. Stop this waste!

"Be filled with the Spirit" (5:18). The form of the verb "fill" is in the middle voice in the original language. The middle voice means the subject is personally involved. Here it means that becoming spiritually fulfilled is not something that happens automatically. The recipient is committed to a new source of motivation for his actions. Paul effectively contrasts the motivation and satisfaction one could receive from two different stimuli. The first method, drunkenness, is artificial and chemical in-filling. The second is spiritual. The first has no real substance and is essentially a wasting experience. The second is truly satisfying.

Spiritual stimulation is totally different in nature. The responsive believer has learned to depend on a source that satisfies the deeper needs of the soul. This source of strength is compatible with his new nature. It would be inappropriate for him to return to the phony, artificial, old life. What used to "fill" him will only leave him empty now. Only God can satisfy his new appetite.

Under God's Control

To be "filled" is a deliberate play on words. The drunkard tried to fill his life by filling himself with wine. It didn't work; it wasted him. The Christian looks for a different sort of in-filling. The language here is metaphorical, of course. The Spirit is not some liquid.

129

The words translated "fill" and "full" in the New Testament suggest being dominated or influenced by something so that you become wholly engaged or involved in it. Tabitha, for example, in Acts 9:36 is "full of good works." This does not mean that an autopsy would have disclosed good works scattered about in her inner anatomy. It means that good works dominated her life. She was under the influence of doing good.

"Fill" can also suggest that a personal agency may be involved in this influence. Peter in Acts 5:3 says to Ananias, "Why has Satan filled your heart to lie to the Holy Spirit?" Ananias was totally under Satan's influence in his deceitful scheme. The alcohol or drug-ridden person is taken over by an addiction. He is the slave, it is the master. The Spirit-filled person depends upon God. The will of God becomes his desire. He is under the influence of God. God controls him. If there is an effective indwelling, the fruit of the Spirit can be produced (Gal. 5:22-23).

"Christ provides a way for us to be filled with what is good and productive, not wasteful."

The contrast in motivation Paul refers to is a choice between the hedonistic life represented by Dionysius, an important diety figure in Greek religion we referred to earlier, and the responsible life headed by Christ.

Dionysius stands for the irrational view of man. He encouraged Mardi-gras type events and orgies where people were encouraged to "let themselves go" and "live it up." Christ, by contrast, was represented to the pagan world as the Son of God who asked for responsible discipleship from his followers. Christ's spiritual influence is contrary to "being drunken with wine." Christ brings the possibility of being liberated from the slavery of "doing our own thing."

Influential philosopher Nietzche recommended that Dionysius became the god of modern man. He meant, of course, man should not take the God of the Bible seriously, but let go of his inhibitions. What religion he had would be Dionysian, a frenzied flight into unreality. So, Dionysius is a dangerous god, as Euripides recognizes in his play, *The Bacchae*. Under his influence a person could commit almost any excess and excuse it.

We have observed a revival of this Dionysian religion in secular hedonism. Still another movement with Dionysian overtones is the attempt to make the Holy Spirit the leader of a cult of spontaneous excess. Such a mistaken thrust is totally pagan in nature. To be filled with the Spirit, rather than being in some mindless frenzy, is to be in one's right mind for the first time.

The contrast Paul points to between the Spirit and the life-wasting effects of drunkenness must not be blurred. Identifying the Spirit with loss of rationality is moving backward. God's Spirit will never be active in someone on a subjective ego-trip. Yet, there is the in-filling of the Spirit which must never be denied. To do so is to totally depart from Christianity (Romans 8). The spiritual person is the one who best realizes the blessings of God in company with the church. He praises God for this with rational song.

The Singing Believer

The individual filled with wine might sing, but with a thick tongue and maudlin words. The one "filled with the Spirit" will "speak in psalms, hymns, and spiritual songs (odes)" (5:19).[1] There is a big difference. The spiritual person does not squander the precious joy of song. He shares it with all God's people in worship. The spiritual person enjoys singing with his fellow believers in an attitude of timeless gratefulness to the Lord Jesus (5:20).

The drinker of alcohol must be with his special buddies and under the influence of booze before he has an urge to sing. The Christian is motivated to sing by the sheer joy of beholding the presence of the worshipping congregation. He is under a high and holy influence. Christians sing because of what they have become through God's grace. It is a grateful song. The joy of union in Christ calls for an appropriate response — a song.

They are "speaking to one another . . ." (5:19). The participle "speaking" is plural, suggesting all sing. The church of Jesus is a portable group not wedded to a building, nor to virtuoso-viewing. The church avoids the spectator syndrome. We do not attend performances — we worship. Jesus taught the portability of the church: "Neither in this mountain nor in Jerusalem shall men worship the Father" (John 4:21ff). God is not confined to a special place, nor does worship depend on specialists or virtuosity. We, the church, are God's organs. Out of our hearts the melody must flow (5:19). It must flow to the Lord, not to appreciative audiences.

Remember how our very birth into the light was surrounded in song (5:14).

'In Everything Give Thanks (5:20)

It may be almost impossible to avoid some trends in singing, but we should be wary of getting away from a spirit of gratefulness (5:20). Sometimes our singing emphasizes only one aspect of Christianity. We may emphasize "going to heaven" songs or concentrate on "toiling on" type songs which focus on the congregation, not Christ. It is easy to be so captured with blessings that no time is left to thank the giver.

The spiritual man relates to his brothers and sisters in God-praising song. He sees the sharing of praise, not as an obligatory performance, but as conversation-in-song that promotes the spirituality of the whole church. Often, unimaginative song selection and unenthusiastic participation dull the positive effects singing can and should have. It is always a problem when people look at worship as a routine.

In the middle ages it was difficult for the abbots of monasteries to ensure that their monks stayed awake and participated satisfactorily in the rote singing. Religious services had become such a duty that all the true beauty and inspiration of praise had dissipated. So some abbot "invented" a junior devil named Tittivillus to frighten the monks into attentiveness. A medieval document called *The Myroure of Oure Ladye* relates the strange story:

> We read of a holy Abbot of the order of Citeaux that while he stood in the choir at matins he saw a fiend that had a long and great poke hanging about his neck and went about the choir from one to another and waited busily after all letters and syllables and words and failings that any made; and them he gathered diligently and put them in his poke. And when he came before the Abbot, waiting if aught had escaped him that he might have gotten and put in his bag, the Abbot was astonied and afeard of the foulness and misshape of him and said unto him: What art thou? And he answered and said, I am a poor devil and my name is Tittivillus and I do mine office that is committed unto me. And what is thine office? said the Abbot. He answered: I must each day, he said, bring my master a thousand pokes full of failings and negligences and syllables and words, that are done in your order in reading and singing and else I must be sore beaten.

If such a creature existed, could he find many wasted words to collect in modern worship services? How tragic if worship in song must be motivated by such low-grade tactics. The spiritual man has a song in his heart. He has seen the light and it has lightened his heart.

The Christian who is in the light is a joyous, thankful worshipper. The light has shown him the new way, and it continues to illuminate his life and point him onward to the radiant presence of his Lord.

Servant 11

What riches exist for us in right relationships! The spiritual man should be concerned for others. Paul says to the spiritual person: "Be in submission to one another in respect for Christ" (5:21).[1] This thought links the activities of the spiritually-minded Christian with his relationships. The connection is more obvious than we might think. The person who is right in his spiritual nature will be most concerned with making relationships work.

Much of our time is invested in making, breaking, or sustaining relationships. The will to relate is one of the strongest drives possessed by humans. We need other people in order to enjoy what we are or what we have. Most people would get little enjoyment out of a new car or a new house if no one ever saw it. Part of the joy of achievement lies in sharing it with others who appreciate it. The burden of sorrow is considerably lightened if others are there to care about us. Our activities gain extra meaning if we have someone to share them with.

Our hunger for relationships, our will to relate, can become so intense that we try to take shortcuts. We approve of any association if it helps avoid isolation and the pain of aloneness. Paul guides the Christian away from such dangers. We distort our ability to recognize true relationships when we enter into false, unstable ones. There are no shortcuts to quality relationships.

The Servant Spirit (5:21)

Basic to the establishment of quality relationships is an altered attitude. God lets us know that the quality of a relationship is directly proportional to the responsible attitudes we bring it. A new Christian is not only transformed individually, he is transformed toward others.

In his pre-Christ days he may have acted toward others as the Gentile rulers mentioned by Jesus in Luke 22:24-27. These rulers styled themselves as "benefactors" (do-gooders). Yet they exercised an exploitative, ruthless control over their subjects. "That's not the way it will be with you . . .," Jesus says (Luke 22:26).[1] The Lord rules out all arbitrary, exploitative authority. He continues, "I am in your midst as one who serves" (Luke 22:27).[1]

The parallel passage in Matthew also emphasizes the nature of authority and relationships under Jesus. "The Son of Man did not come to be served but to serve and give his life as a ransom in the stead of many" (Matt. 20:28).[1]

The basic note of the new attitude in relationships is *service*. Paul says, "Be in submission to one another in respect for Christ" (5:21).[1] Respect for Christ's new insights on the nature of relationships causes the believer to change his attitude. He surrenders his ego-centered desire for dominance in the relationship and accepts the role of one who serves. The word "respect" is the same in the original of 5:21 and 5:33. It is a noun in 5:21 and a verb in 5:33 and is correctly translated "respect" in both contexts.

Christ did not come to feed anyone's ego. He came to serve and teach others to serve. Paul refers to respect for Christ because Christ's attitude is a radical departure from the way most relationships are maintained. People often accept either a dominant or passive role. Some energetically fight for dominance. Others submit reluctantly to what they think is a superior force. Only in Christ is there the liberating desire to serve others' needs.

Christ set into motion the new attitude toward relationships. He accepted his role of service. Respect for Christ's example forms the motive for our new attitudes about people. Those in Christ do not relate according to the latest pop sociology movement, nor by avante-garde "liberation" movements. Believers are motivated by respect for Christ's effective method of structuring relationships so that they are of the greatest benefit to those involved.

Submitting Self

But what does it mean to "submit to one another" (5:21)?[1] The word "submit" occurs frequently in the New Testament. No arbitrary or non-contextual meaning should be assigned. Only an overview of several passages helps us see the meaning.

Submission occurs in 1 Corinthians 16:16. The Corinthians are called upon to submit themselves to believers with a record of service like Stephanus. What could this mean? Were the Corinthians to bow to whatever whim Stephanus or people like him could think up? Obviously not. People like Stephanus did not engage in whimsical behavior. The Corinthians were to assist in supplying the needs of such remarkable servants. Here submission means a readiness to meet the needs of people.

Younger men are asked to be submissive to older men (1 Pet. 5:5). The context indicates this is a readiness to recognize their superior experience and wisdom when they act as competent examples. Peter certainly could not mean that young men are to submit to any whimsical or foolish demand solely because it comes from an older person. Would this benefit anyone?

The principle is beginning to emerge. Submission, in the New Testament context, is a responsible action, not the acceptance of whimsical, exploitative directions. This is obvious in 1 Peter 2:13[1]. Peter commands Christians to be "in submission to every human institution." (E.G. Selwyn says Peter means to "be subject to every fundamental social institution.") Christians are not rebels. They support stability in society.

It doesn't take much insight to see the limitation that wisdom would apply to this injunction. Peter recognized the limits of human authority when he said to the rulers in Jerusalem who had commanded a stop to gospel preaching: "We must obey God rather

138

than men" (Acts 5:29). Service to religious leaders in Jerusalem could not replace loyalty to God. So, by saying "be subject one to another," Paul is not demanding some sort of senseless response to arbitrary behavior. He appeals for the transformation of relationships made possible only by service. When we submit, it indicates respect for Christ and a serious desire to serve.

Serving One Another (5:22)

The best texts of Ephesians 5:22 contain no main verb. The verb "be in submission"[1] comes from verse 21. The command to be "in submission to one another" finds its fulfillment in each relationship listed after the theme statement (5:21).[1] Husbands and wives, parents and children, masters and slaves, each has a responsibility to serve the needs of others. Each submits to that service out of respect for Christ. Subjection and submission are virtually synonymous, interchangeable terms.

Subjection is not a one-way proposition. Men must be submissive, too. How can this work? How can a husband subject himself to his wife and still have his wife submit to him? He submits as he accepts his responsibility to be the head of the wife in the spirit of Christ. A spirit of service, not dominance. He serves her needs.

The wife, in turn, submits herself out of respect for Christ. She permits her husband to fulfill his God-given responsibility. This serves his needs and helps him become what he should be in the relationship. He graciously accepts this burden of service, and she serves by supporting him in his responsible decision.

There are no shortcuts to quality relationships, especially marriage. Marriage is God's idea for mankind. God knew it was unnatural for man to live alone. God, therefore, created a relationship where men and women could share at the deepest levels of their being. It can only be a quality relationship when the God who originated it dominates it. True happiness cannot come without a committed relationship.

In spite of all its failures and frustrations, marriage still offers responsible men and women a tremendous opportunity to enter into a "oneness" not found at any other level. God offers marriage to man and woman so they may know each other in the most intimate form of togetherness. Marriage as created by God gives the man-woman relationship a stability it could never possess otherwise. Paul explains how marriage will work best. He reveals the directions of its originator — God. That means going in with the servant attitude of Christ.

The Price of Headship (5:23)

Christ is the head of the church (5:23). Every member of his body owes respect to Christ. The wife submits to her husband, who is compared to Christ in his position as head of the church. To help understand what this means we must answer two questions: How did Christ come to be head of the church? How does he maintain that position?

Suppose some foolish person were to ask: "Did Christ become head of the church by seizing power in some divine *coup de etat*?" "Ridiculous," we would answer. We know that was not his method of assuming this responsibility. We know he became head of the church by earning that right by his sacrificial action at the cross on behalf of each of us. So, at the outset we know the nature of Christ's authority is not that of a power seizure.

Christ's headship is the *result* of responsible loving action. Paul realized that the Philippians would never act responsibly toward one another until they started to think in the same way that Christ thinks (Phil. 2:5). How does Christ think? Paul's answer indicates that Christ does not concentrate on what private rights may accrue to himself, but on how he may serve.

Christ did not insist on holding onto his divine perogatives. When he saw a greater good would come to us from emptying himself, this is what he did. He accepted the form of a servant (Phil. 2:7). He died a cross-death, not an ordinary death. "Therefore," Paul says, *then and only then* did his exaltation come (Phil. 2:9). The way to sovereignty was through sacrifice and surrender. Paul refers to this when he says "as Christ is the head of the church. . . ." No whimsical, arbitrary authority, but one which comes to exist, continues to exist, and is based on sacrificial service.

The Marriage Process (5:24)

What is an ideal wife? Booth Tarkington's clever response neatly answers the question: "An ideal wife is any woman who has an ideal husband." This hits it exactly. You can never consider the duties of the wife apart from the husband, nor the husband apart from the wife. This passage is a good illustration of the dynamic, process nature of interrelationship that marriage is (5:22-23). Is the wife called on to submit to the husband (5:24)? Yes. But the husband is instructed to love and serve his wife as Christ did the church (5:21, 25ff).

Can the wife submit to a husband who will not love her as Christ loved the church? How could she? How could we submit to Christ if Christ had not loved us, entered the world on our behalf, suffered for us, and on that basis made a claim on our obedience? What would we submit to? What would our relationship with such a Christ be? It would certainly be far different from the relationship we can now have because Christ loves us.

Of course, even if her husband were irresponsible, the Christian wife would still act responsibly herself. In this way she could serve his needs and give him a model of Christian character (1 Pet. 3:1-6). Nevertheless, unless they were "joint heirs of grace" (1 Pet. 3:7)[1] the relationship would be far from what God intended it to be.

"This submission does not suggest inferiority because the husband and wife are both submitting."

On the other hand, how effective could a husband's love be for a nonsubmitting wife? Would not his attempts at a sacrificial caring love be frustrated by a dominating, power-desiring wife? Christ's love for us would prove fruitless if we failed to submit to him. But when the husband follows Christ's model of love, he makes it possible for the wife to submit to his responsible direction.

This submission does not suggest inferiority because the husband and wife are both submitting. He submits to her needs in accepting responsibility for the direction of the relationship. She submits to his direction so that he may love her sacrificially and productively.

Nothing inferior in women is mentioned. This passage does not say that women are incompetent to direct people or affairs. The famous passage on wives (Prov. 31:10ff) portrays an extremely competent woman as ideal. In the relationship called marriage, God calls on the husband to serve by accepting overall responsibility.

What is the believing wife to do if she has a husband who will not act responsibly? It will be difficult for her to submit because the husband's lack of responsibility is evidence of his lack of love for her. This type of submission is not bowing to the will of an emotional ogre. We must reject this interpretation of submission. Instead of playing at whim-satisfaction, the wife must do what is possible to get the husband to act responsibly. She must remember that the will of God has precedence over the will of the husband.

One author, in a popular book on the Christian family, carries his idea of wifely submission to the point of encouraging whim-satisfaction. He actually advises the Christian wife to stop attending church services if her husband orders her to. This would be a sin against God as well as severely disruptive of the salvation relationship the wife has with Jesus. Marriage ends with the death of the marriage partner, but our relationship with Jesus never ends. In the final analysis, God has priority.

The Giving Husband (5:25-27)

The husband who wants a submissive wife must carefully consider his response (5:22-33). Primarily, the husband is called upon to be an active lover. This may seem like a strange way to move toward responsibility, but it is Christ's way. Loving means far more than romantic or sexual love, as important as they are. The love called for here is sacrificial, goal-centered, and personal. These are the guideposts of a love which help the wife submit to being served in such a wonderful way.

The husband must be a sacrificial lover (5:25): "Husbands, love your wives just as Christ loved the church and gave himself over on her behalf."[1] The essence of love is giving, not receiving. A husband must head off any ideas of his wife being there merely to satisfy his personal ego desires. He must perceive his wife's needs and act to meet them by giving of himself. If Christ had only been thinking of his own welfare, he would not have given himself. We would have no relationship with him. So the nongiving husband cannot expect any sort of viable relationship with his wife. At best, she will be a ghostly echo of his own desires.

A wife is not an unpaid servant. She is a person to be loved. We must learn to use things and love people, not love things and use people. Many marriages flounder at this point. A comic verse typifies the attitude of many nongiving husbands:

> He wrecked his car, he lost his job
> And yet, throughout his life,
> He took his troubles like a man:
> He blamed them on his wife.

144

What is it that Christ gave anyway? Possessions? Advice? No. He gave himself (5:25). The husband who gives himself will have a wife who can readily submit to such service. His "I provide for you" is now included under the larger heading of "I love you."

The husband must love with a goal-centered love. Many marriages are like unmerry merry-go-rounds. No real goal exists for the relationship! But Christ's love has a purpose; it's not a romantic daydream. He wants us to be pure and holy. He desires these goals for us as a result of our conversion (5:26-27). He knew our limitations and had no illusions about what we were; yet he still had a design for our relationship with him.

The husband is to love his wife in the same realistic way. He knows she has faults, as he does. His love has purpose though. He desires, as Christ does for the church, that the relationship move toward what is better. The husband should see that the marriage does not deteriorate. He should take the lead in keeping the relationship alive and moving.

The wife should not have to spend all of her time appealing for communication, concern, and interest to be expressed. How can she submit to a husband who does not work to make the relationship grow? I recall counseling with a couple with a problem like that. The wonder and excitement had been snuffed out of their marriage because they were no longer looking for new territory to explore together. There are such depths to be discovered in persons if we don't abandon the search. Submission will be endangered if the husband does not love with a goal-centered love.

As You Love Yourself (5:23-30)

The husband is also instructed to be personally involved in his love for his wife. Nothing is more personal than our own bodies. Husbands are to love their wives "as their own bodies" (5:28). This challenge is for love to be immediate, not by remote control. A husband must not place his wife on an impersonal pedestal, but be involved with her as a human being. A wife should be loved as a person, not a sex object nor a beautiful possession.

A wife is another self. It's like loving yourself to love your wife, Paul says (5:28). To deny love to your wife is actually to deny love to yourself. This indicates that a man who cannot love his wife probably is incapable of loving himself. A story tells of an obstetrician who determined his fees in an unusual way. If a man emerged from the waiting room after his baby's birth and asked, "Is it a boy or girl?" the doctor sent a bill for $200. If the husband asked, "How is my wife?" he got a bill for $100.

Christ considers a good relationship worth keeping (5:29). What a pity men and women are so ready to throw away good relationships for romantic illusions or to spite the marriage partner. A good brother in tears called me one night. His wife had left him for another man. Many years of companionship were being thrown away. What makes us think anything will last without working at it? Christ works at making our relationship with him permanent. We need to take a similar view.

Magnum Mysterium (5:31-33)

Paul sums it up! Love and respect go hand in hand (5:33). Respect will not exist if no love is present.

Love breeds respect. We have come full circle. It was respect for Christ that led us to submit to the needs of one another (5:21). Now we see that respect grows when we perceive love. How many marital failures would be headed off by following this course of action?

Christians should see this whole passage; not only as a way to personal happiness, but a great opportunity to demonstrate the practicality of the Lord's ways. The world is watching.

Paul returns to the basic intention of marriage by quoting from Genesis 2:24. The man is called on again to take responsible action. He should take the lead in committing himself to his wife: leaving parents and clinging to his wife. This affirms the nature of the husband's leadership. He must take the radical action of placing loyalty to his wife before loyalty to all else but God.

The care and concern Christ has for the church is a profound mystery. The closest comparison Paul makes is the marriage encounter. Marriage can draw its life from this comparison. Christ left all to devote himself to our needs. He still "clings" to us. When we follow this radical action of Christ we will know the meaning of service.

Respect 12

Children in today's space age are exposed to an almost unlimited barrage of data. Travel to the moon seems commonplace. The dubious blare of tv provides young minds with a thousand and one sights and delights, some good, some indifferent, many evil. The outbreak of war in some remote corner of the world threatens to bring sophisticated death machines whirring out of the soundless skies. There seems to be a shortage of everything except crises and corruption. What does the Bible say to space-age children?

Children and parents are often near strangers. Both parents are probably pursuing their own destinies while substitutes raise their children. Even parents who try to communicate with their children find them locked into the goosestep conformity of peer-group pressure. Parents feel confused, useless, and helpless. Children float around, the hapless debris of disintegrated relationships. What does the Bible say to modern parents?

This passage speaks about human relationships, especially modern parents and children (6:1-9). It gives us a view of a home established upon God's principles. These principles enable the home to win the struggle for identity and build a foundation based on Christ, not on the changing whims of society and culture. The dominant forces today are disruptive and disintegrative. Paul recognizes that only Christ's strength can counter these centrifugal forces.

Space-age Children (6:1)

"Children, obey your parents in the Lord, for this is right" (Eph. 6:1). Before we apply this principle to our children, we need to respect them as persons. Here is where we face a problem, though, for while we indulge our children we often do not know them. Recently on a popular tv show a mother was offered $8,000 if she could guess whether her preteen daughter would chose a space suit or a cowgirl outfit when the choice was offered to her. The mother confidently said the child would choose the space suit. But her daughter instantly picked the cowgirl outfit. Our lack of knowledge can be more harmful than this. To respect someone, we must take the time to know what the world looks like from their viewpoint.

Parents often assume that childhood is a happy, carefree time. They tell young people: "This is the happiest time of your life . . . Enjoy it while you can." This is not only highly inaccurate, but downright misleading. Misleading because it

149

suggests that adulthood is a worry-filled time of dreary drudgery.

Parents may reflect their own pessimistic view of life, but why infect a child with the virus of our discontent? This parental assumption is inaccurate because it presupposes youth to be a time of carefree happiness. Actually young people are quite insecure because they are experiencing many changes in their lives. Physical and emotional changes are normal for this age group. A teenage girl can be devastated by the overnight appearance of a pimple on her nose. Things trivial to adults crush young people.

Young people of today are also under enormous pressure from their peer groups. Some children are emotionally shattered by peer group disapproval. They knuckle under like the boy who described his conformity to the group by saying: "I came, I saw, and I concurred." The group reinforces the security of the child, and it can be mindless and destructive. Christian parents must know the members of their children's group. This is also a part of knowing them.

A most destructive tendency in our world today, one that every parent should be wary of, is the cult of youthfulness. The world worships the idea of being young, but at the same time it can actually despise young people. George Bernard Shaw remarked, "Youth is a wonderful thing; it's too bad it's wasted on young people." Even the apparently placid Timothy had those of his own faith who were ready to despise his youth (1 Tim. 4:12). Parents can divert this strange hostility by supporting the young person as a person of worth.

A home will grow toward Christ when the parents take time to know their children and the influences they face. In this passage (6:1-4) we discover a mutual respect and obligation between parents and children that does not exist in the secular world. This is the perspective we must search for in restoring stability to the home: respect for persons.

Mutual Respect

The contrast between the apostolic mentality in this passage, with its emphasis upon mutual obligations, and the attitude of the surrounding pagan world is striking. The callous disregard for life seen in our own culture was doubly present in Paul's day. Christians were distinguished by their respect for life and their opposition to the disregard for personhood so prevalent then.

A letter written in the first century A.D. illustrates the pagan attitude toward children. Hilarion is writing his wife Alis (Papyri Number 744.9). Freely translated, the letter says: "If you should after a time give birth, if it happens to be a boy, keep him. If it's a girl, expose her." The casual cruelty of this letter is unspeakably horrible. This is how far a culture falls when God is ignored as the Creator of personhood and Father of all mankind. The Christian approach to the home begins with respect for life.

Respect for the new life God has given to a man and woman is the motivation for Christian child-rearing. Paul calls upon the child to carry on this motivation by respecting his parents, who also show respect for him! That is why he begins: "Children, obey your parents in the Lord, for this is right" (6:1). In other words, Paul says to the heirs of this great tradition of respect for personhood: "In the Lord there is a right way to act at every condition and stage of life. As children of Christian parents, you must obey them."

"In the Lord" is a common expression in Greek. It means "in the sphere of the Lord's direction." The Lord intended for children to obey their parents, even if the parents are irresponsible.

Doing the Right Thing (6:2-3)

Within the range of "submitting to one another" (5:21), parents serve the best interests of their children by accepting responsibility for their direction and education. Children are bound "in the Lord" to accept this responsible service and obey their parents. Obedience is the "right thing to do" (6:1-2).[1] But our culture does not insist on this attitude.

An oriental visitor, when asked about the most amazing thing he had observed in America, replied: "I was amazed at how well American parents obey their children." Most observant! We have all suffered from the fallout of a permissive society. And children have not learned self-control and respect.

We may plead extenuating circumstances. We blame our mobile society for the uprooting of home and neighborhood. We blame our urban culture for robbing children of character-building manual work of the farm. Peer pressure and absentee parents are other excuses, and on and on the list goes. We need to cut through all these excuses, and go to the child, and say: "In the Lord there is a right way to act.

152

That means obedience and respect for parents. We insist on this behavior." Simplistic? Yes, but most quality solutions are. (Parents must also respect their children. If it's disrespectful for children to yell at parents, then parents should avoid screaming at their children.)

But can we get this message out to the world in general? One religious group has had great success with some simple family tv spots and this bumper sticker: "Have You Hugged Your Kid Today?" Mass media messages have some value, but the best demonstration occurs simply by watching the Christian home itself. The world would quickly discover a secret: obedient children are secure, happy children. Not only that, they have learned the invaluable lesson of respect for other persons.

"Respect for the new life God has given to a man and woman is the motivation for Christian child-rearing."

Obedience, you see, grows out of "honoring father and mother" (6:2).[1] Respect is the root of obedience. Respect and obedience create stability and a state of well-being in the child who knows the source of his direction.

Harmonious home relationships promote well-being and healthy emotions (6:3). Considering the obvious connection between emotional and physical well-being, these relationships also promote good health. When responsible parents

153

creatively direct their children, the children do not have to assume a responsibility they are not ready to handle. They can grow and develop without anxieties and emotional traumas which haunt children who rebel and strike out on their own.

Sometimes, of course, even responsible parents encounter disobedient children. Other influences dominate the lives of these young people. Remember the experience of God and the man and woman in the Garden of Eden? Surely no one would charge God with negligence in his instructions to Adam and Eve. Yet they rebelled. They permitted an alien influence to dominate their lives, casting a bad reflection on themselves, not the Creator.

When parents have prayerfully done their duty in the Lord they should not be tormented by guilt when a child rebels. They must maintain a stance like the father in the parable of the prodigal son. The son or daughter *must return* before they can be accepted. When they return they *must be* accepted.

Frustrated Children (6:4)

Paul balances the call for children's obedience with a demand upon parents: "You fathers, stop frustrating your children, but nourish them in the education and instruction of the Lord (6:4)."[1] Present-day pessimism about family life indicates raising children is not easy. A recent unscientific poll by a newspaper columnist revealed about 70 percent of those responding regretted having had children. Disappointed parents are probably resentful.

People are so busy with their search for personal freedom that children get in the way. The little ones infringe on the supposed rights of selfish parents. Christian parents have a rare opportunity to show that raising a child is not a third-class vocation, but a beautifully creative God-sent gift.

Paul tells fathers to stop frustrating their children. "Fathers" often occurs in Greek literature to mean "parents" and that may be the meaning here. Paul believes parental frustration stops growth.

What are some common ways parents frustrate their children? A questionnaire given recently to a class of about thirty-five junior high young people revealed some interesting answers. One ninth grader said she loved her parents, but they often gave her an automatic "no" to almost any request she made. When queried by the youngster, her parents' only reply was, "That's the way it is." Of course, many children do not understand or appreciate the reasons parents give, but many young people did say they understood the reason "later." But this does illustrate a particularly frustrating method of dealing with children.

Parents themselves would not appreciate this kind of treatment from others. Anyone who has encountered a tight-lipped government official or a worker who offers no reasons or explanations for his actions can appreciate the frustrations involved.

The survey also revealed another concern to children. They are deeply disturbed by parents' inconsistencies in dealing with all children in the home. Young people are particularly sensitive to fair play and equal access to parental approval. One girl said she was forbidden to do a certain activity which her sister was allowed to do. Her parents told her she would be able to do the same thing when she was old as her sister. The younger sister said, "She has been doing it for years, even when she was my age." But her parents wouldn't even discuss the inconsistency. Parents should not fear admitting their mistakes. They must be honest with their children if they want their children to be honest with them!

Most of the frustrations are caused by poor communication. Paul Tournier was certainly right, "Most conversations are dialogues of the deaf." Sincere listening should be a first-rate priority for parents. Almost every young person in the class said: "My parents don't listen to me! They don't take time to hear my side of the story." Parents need to learn the skill of listening.

The biological act of bearing children does not automatically equip parents with the ability to raise children. Principles of active listening, sympathetic treatment, and fairness do not violate good disciplinary procedure. In fact, they assist in good discipline. Children are people and people must be given attention and respect. Parents should not resent spending time acquiring these skills.

Tending the Garden

What is needed? Nourishment. Not just good food, though that's necessary, but spiritual nourishment. Paul says, "Nourish them in the education and instruction of the Lord" (vs. 4).[1] The nourishing of children is not mind-control. Nourishment is designed to draw out the best potential in the child.

Nourishing is like tending a garden. No human can create a plant. But he can tend them. Parents brought the child into existence by God's creative action. This new person is theirs, not to control, but to nourish. Parents can tend a garden. They can spot and remove weeds that would choke out good growth. They can apply correct stimulation to the spirit of the child so that healthy growth may occur. They can accept their task as one of nourishment.

Consider the word translated "education" in this verse. It is frequently translated "discipline," but this translation has so many negative meanings in English it is better to translate *paideia* as "education." It means more than "discipline." In ancient Greece the word meant the whole spectrum of cultural and educational influences acting on the child's life. The word is often accompanied in Greek literature with the adjective "all-encircling." *Paideia* was comprehensive, touching every aspect of life, not merely the school room.

Paul was familiar with this concept. He mentions his "education" at the feet of the noted teacher Gamaliel in Acts 22:3, using the same word in verb form he used in Ephesians 6:4 in noun form *(paideia)*. Paul's home city, Tarsus, was highly regarded as an education center in the ancient world. Strabo, the ancient geographer, comments on Tarsus:

> The people at Tarsus have devoted themselves so eagerly, not only to philosophy, but also to the whole round of education *(paideia)* in general that they have surpassed Athens, Alexandria, and any other place that can be named . . . .

Now Paul advises that education also be conducted "in the Lord."

We might think the word "education" means turning our child over to some expert. But this is not what Paul means. H.I. Marrou, a highly regarded scholar in the field of ancient education, says in *Education in Antiquity:*

> . . . The early church would have had sharp words to say about "Christian" parents of today who think that they have done all that is required of them when they have passed their children over to a teacher or an institution (p. 419).

Marrou is right. Education begins in the home. If Christian education is not there, it may not matter if it occurs elsewhere.

We should be grateful for the many fine Christian educational institutions. But there is no substitute for a Christian education which begins in the home. The family remains God's basic structure for shaping, directing, and instructing the character of a child. That is why parental devotion to the family is a far nobler activity than any career which brings "self expression."

Growing Whole Children

Secular education is often one-sided. Even an educated person is apt to be an intellectual giant, but a spiritual dwarf. The concept of *paideia* stresses a well-rounded person. A person with only a secular viewpoint is not well-educated. This is why we have problems with morality and ethics today. The spiritual dimension is totally neglected in most children's lives. Pindar, the ancient Theban poet of the fifth century B.C., catches the problem neatly in these lines:

A man can learn and yet see darkly
Blow one way, then another,
Walking ever on uncertain feet,
His mind unfinished and fed with scraps of a
thousand virtues.

A mind without a spiritual dimension is an "unfinished mind."

Instruction in the Lord

To "education" Paul adds "instruction" (*nouthesia*). The literal meaning is "placing in the mind." The instruction of the lord is the placing of those guiding education principles into the child's mind. Education is the curriculum, instruction is the implementation. Parents must have a plan to implement the valuable principles of God's word. Congregations should help parents equip themselves with the required skills.

When education and instruction is conducted "in the Lord" with Christ as center, true maturity is possible (Col. 1:28).[1] Our world desperately needs mature persons. Only Christ makes this possible. Christian parents can restore some sanity to the planet if they take their responsibilities seriously.

Submit to the Master (6:5-9)

The unspeakable horror of slavery was a fact of life in Paul's time. This passage and others indicate that many believers were slaves. Should the slave seek a political or revolutionary solution to his problem? Paul says they should seek a heart solution: The slave in honest workmanship and the master in willing recognition of the existence of a higher Master were to learn submission to the Lord. This is the wedge that eventually broke the power of slavery.

Many bloody slave revolutions failed to win freedom for slaves. A tremendous outbreak by slaves in Sicily was put down by Rome with great loss of life. Spartacus recruited an army of 90,000 escaped slaves and nearly crushed Italy, but Crassus crucified 6,000 of them along the Appian Way and broke the revolt. Only Christ gave an ultimate bloodless victory to these defenseless human beings.

Historians estimate that from one-quarter to one-third of the people in the Roman Empire were slaves. Slaves had no rights, though some masters were better than others. A slave's wife, children, and other relatives could be sold and shipped away at the will of the master. In Rome every slave in a household could be killed if one slave killed the master, and this happened on several occasions. Even the genial Aristotle spoke of slaves as no better than "speaking tools."

The message of Christ came as a great liberating force to these slaves. Why? Because the message of the cross said all were equal in sin, all could have access to grace through the cross! God's own son loved slaves enough to die for them. Emperor, senator, praetor, Roman knight, plebian, slave — all were sinners in need of Christ's mercy. Only the cross could redeem.

Truly the ground is level at the foot of the cross. This is the greatest principle of equality ever announced. Once it gets into the human heart no exploitation of another human being can survive very long. This eventually broke the back of slavery.

Respecting Subordinates

Ephesians 6:5-9 is valuable for the Christian worker (6:5-9). Instead of dishonest loafing at the water cooler or on coffee break, the Christian works responsibly as unto Christ (6:5). The believer does not butter up the boss and play office politics to get ahead. He advances by enthusiastic work as if he is serving the Lord.

Sometimes the best thing we can do for Christ is put in an honest day's work. You can hand out tracts by the millions to your fellow workers telling all about Christ and the church. But if they know you as a shirker, your life will keep getting in the way of your teaching. A Christian needs a sense of mission in his work, as well as other areas of his life.

Employers can also profit from Paul's discussion. Threatening people is no way to gain their cooperation. Many bosses intimidate, belittle, and otherwise dominate their employees. A Christian boss may think he has to do this to keep up with his worldly competitors. But fair and equitable treatment of subordinates generates excellent morale in workers. A happy worker works better.

General Douglas MacArthur reportedly gave his superiors difficulty at times, but he never mistreated a subordinate. This is a mark of nobility. Christ's people remain humble, no matter how many serve under them. They are aware of One always above them to whom they are responsible.

161

A computerized assembly line may seem a long way from the solitary craftsmen of Paul's day. "Things are different now," we say. "No one really works directly for another. There are middlemen, wheeler-dealers, agents. It's just not the same." Paul would probably say to all this: "Doing right is still doing right." Even a middleman can work for the Lord and maintain his personal integrity.

Think how much a true restoration of ethics would mean to consumers today. How much ethical power would surface if every Christian businessman, car salesman, factory worker, and office worker would work "unto the Lord!"

The riches we receive from Christ shine brightly in these passages on relationships. The Lord's guidance extends deeply into his dealings with fellow human beings. Men and women in Christ can find all the fulfillment marriage offers. Parents and children can have a loving, character-building association. Christ brings rich relationships.

Struggle 13

"Finally, be strong in the Lord and in the strength of his might" (6:10). "Finally" we have reached the bottom line, as businessmen are so fond of saying. We have reached the point of decision. Now it is time to take a stand. All doctrine, all life, all that is affirmed in Christ come to the testing point. It must be that way. Faith and discipleship are not academic concerns, but confrontations. Confrontations with the malignant evil that blights the lives of countless men and women. A stand must be made. The struggle is on.

Paul does not ask that we merely "be strong," but "be strong in the Lord." Too many people try to be strong on their own. Often you hear a well-meaning individual say to someone who is depressed: "Buck up, be strong!" But there is a definite limit to how strong any person can be on his own. It is good stoic doctrine to try to lift yourself by your own spiritual bootstraps, but it is not apostolic doctrine.

This strength we need is not merely for ourselves. The struggle is not merely for the sake of a struggle. There is a spirit of stoicism in some people that seeks self-contained nobility through suffering. The heroes of many Hemingway stories, for example, go out of their way to find wars to fight and bloody encounters with bulls and fish.

Strong in the Lord (6:10-11)

Being strengthened in the Lord is a continuing process because the verb "be strong" is present tense (6:10). The Lord's power sustains us in our struggle, but we still must "put on the whole armor of God" (6:11). We make a conscious decision to use the protection God makes available. God's whole armor is more like an armory. The word Paul uses for armor *(panoplia)* means the weapons and armor of a soldier or Hoplite — a heavily-armed soldier. We have a virtual arsenal at our disposal!

God does not skimp on the equipment. Without all God's armor, we are defenseless against the devil's clever tactics. Without God's arsenal, we are powerless to mount an offensive for righteousness. This kind of struggle cannot be won on our own. We must put on the whole armor of God, not just the comfortable parts.

Paul says the powers of evil are much stronger than we could imagine. We may think we are battling only human ideas and human stubbornness, but there are dark forces opposed to God and his people. These powerful forces will easily conquer us unless we have invincible armor at our disposal. If we will but use it!

We will lose the battle and eventually the war if we are caught out on our own with only our own resources. An army cannot win without proper equipment. Even the gallant South under General Robert E. Lee was ultimately powerless against the superior resources of the North. Fortunately, God has supplied us with ample equipment to win a great victory.

Our Struggle (6:12)

Paul says, "Our struggle (contending, RSV) is not against flesh and blood, but with the rulers, the authorities, the world-rulers of this darkness, with the spiritual forces of wickedness in the heavenly spheres" (6:12).[1] Notice he does not say "God's struggle" or "my struggle," but "our struggle." We are all involved.

The sphere of action is "the heavenly spheres." We noticed previously that the struggle is a present reality (1:3, 2:6, 3:10).[1] We are engaged in a heavenly struggle even now. Our struggle has eternal implications. It is not an earthly war at all. The call is not to a crusade to recover territory on this earth. It is not an inquisition to ferret out the heretics and literally or figuratively burn them at the stake. It is not a struggle "against flesh and blood" at all.

Our struggle is possible because at last we know who the real enemy is — the satanic powers of darkness. Men and women may be taken prisoners to do the will of the evil one (2 Tim. 2:26). Yet they are not our enemies. The struggle is deeper than that.

"Our struggle is not against flesh and blood . . ." William Buckley once said: "Personal hostility should not be a mark of the strength of one's convictions." We are not to be hostile to people, but to evil. Too often "crusaders" for truth actually are motivated by opposition to other people. They have what may be called a "dialectical faith." They see themselves in a struggle, but it is often a struggle against another personality that clashes with theirs. Their faith is defined only in terms of its opposition. Its points and dogmas are images of the opponent's beliefs, defined only by contrasting terms. This person will fight for freedom because his opponent is for slavery. He has no hostility to slavery, only to people who advocate it. He will be for grace, not because he rejoices in God's mercy, but because his opponent is a legalist. We must escape this trap. Believe and practice what is right because it is right, not because people we like agree with us — or people we dislike disagree with us.

"As we accept the discipleship of the cross, we stand with Christ."

"Our struggle" is a call to action. Christianity is not an invitation to relax spiritually, but to struggle to right great wrongs, to adventure, burn, and blow out on the winds of time for Christ Jesus! General Douglas MacArthur said, "In war there is no substitute for victory." There is no substitute for going all out to win the battle against evil. This call to action is a flat denial of the spectator mentality prevalent today.

We are participants. It is "our struggle." Listen to Edmund Burke's eloquent words: "The only thing necessary for the triumph of evil is for good men to do nothing."

Perhaps many of us in the Lord's army have retired on our pension before the struggle is resolved or could we have gone A.W.O.L. from the Lord's army? Do we fit into Matthew Arnold's description of slovenly discipleship in his poem *The Scholar Gypsy:*

Light half-believers of our casual creeds,
Who never deeply felt, nor clearly willed,
Whose insight never has borne fruit in deeds,
Whose vague resolves have never been fulfilled,
For whom each year we see
Breeds new beginnings, disappointments new,
Who hesitate and falter life away,
And lose tomorrow the ground won today.

There is no inactive reserve in the Lord's army.

Take Up (6:13-14)

"Because of this, take up the entire armor of God that you may be able to stand fast in the evil day, and having made every preparation to stand. Stand, therefore . . ." (6:13-14a).[1] For this struggle we need both strength and equipment. We know "strength" is available in the Lord, now we need to add the "equipment." We are going to have to make a stand. Not to decide is to have decided already not to make that stand.

The church of Jesus either takes a stand for him or abandons its place. A cricket club in England recently voted to disband. The reason? "The members lost interest," a spokesman said, explaining that the club had not played a match in 25

167

years. What took them so long to disband? They ceased to exist as a cricket club when they stopped playing cricket.

When churches abandon the struggle for Jesus' cause, they have ceased to exist as churches. Apathy and a "serve-me" mentality are deadly enemies of commitment to Christ. Apathy destroyed the power of the citizenship of republican Rome. Who can forget Juvenal's bitter lines:

The public . . . has flung off its cares;
For the people, who once bestowed authority,
Army commands, Consulships, and all else,
Today keep their hands to themselves,
And for just two things do they eagerly yearn:
Bread and the games.

They sat down never to stand again.

"Stand therefore," Paul says. We are "standing," not only against something, but for something. As we accept the discipleship of the cross, we stand with Christ. We join the most worthwhile cause of all. We are involved in the greatest struggle and the greates victory of all times.

Alexandr Solzhenitsyn's criticism of the Russian church makes this point well: "Russian history might have been incomparably more humane and harmonious in the last few centuries if the church had not surrendered its independence." It is not time for surrender, it is a time to take a stand!

"Take up the whole armor of God. . ." Every item of armor is important. We dare not omit a single item. A soldier with an excellent rifle but no helmet will soon be in trouble. A close inventory of God's armor reveals the necessity for each item in our stand against evil.

Bound with Truth (6:14a)

"Having girded your waist with truth . . ."[1] The girding of one's waist in ancient times meant preparation for activity. Truth is compared to protecting the vital areas of your body.

Truth may be an optional luxury for most persons, or a matter of subjective relativity by philosophers. But to Christians, truth is vital because it reveals the reality about God's will for us. Jesus is the ultimate certification of the existence of truth. "I am the way, the truth, and the life," he affirms (John 14:6).[1]

Truth is not a series of intellectual propositions. The truth of God reveals things the way they really are. To be guarded by the truth means to know both the content and application. We cannot really take a stand for God without using his truth. And just knowing it is not enough, it must surround us ("girded" in 6:14 literally means "to wrap around").

The truth about God causes us to see the truth about ourselves and make the necessary response. Ignoring the truth will not excuse the spiritual disaster which follows. Only a fool would cover the red warning lights on his car so he wouldn't know when his engine was too hot or his oil pressure too low. No matter how painful it may be, we have to stay close to the truth. In this way we can monitor our own closeness to the Lord and help others find truth. Truth is meant for our protection. Truth provides power to counter the subtle temptations of the devil or rescue another human from a web of spiritual deception. It is where we start in preparing ourselves to stand up for what is right.

The Breastplate of Righteousness (6:14b)

"Clothed with the breastplate of righteousness . . . ."[1] The breastplate protects the heart. Righteousness puts truth into operation in our lives. It translates the words of God into the deeds of God in us. Righteousness means (standing in the right) with God. Philippians 3:8-9 affirms the source of righteousness as faith in Christ.

Right-standing with God is available to the one who puts his trust in Jesus (Rom. 3:21-26). Christ is our righteousness (1 Cor. 1:30). How can we even dare to lay our hands on God's armor? Only because we have acquittal with God and right-standing with him by the sacrifice of Christ. We can take our stand alongside him. Our repentant response of faith, which included the creative encounter of baptism, demonstrated our trust in the cross.

We can never take off the breastplate of righteousness! The ancient soldier could remove his armor, but we stay in the right with God by continual dependence on the blood of Jesus. Jesus not only died for us, but he lives for us to ensure our ongoing relationship with God (Rom. 5:9-11). The breastplate of righteousness was formed by the master Workman. His tools were the cross and the open tomb.

The Soldier's Foot Armor (6:15)

"Having your feet shod with readiness for the gospel of peace . . ."[1] This foot armor is designed for more than just protection or appearance. Like the famous seven-league boots, these shoes are designed for action. The Christian does not occupy

170

static ground. He's not in a rut. He advances with the gospel. The best defense is a good offense.

Paul talks about a readiness to spread the gospel of peace. He means that even though the Christian is in a struggle, he still bears a message of peace and reconciliation to mankind. Satan opposes this, but in sharing the gospel we enjoy double protection by operating offensively and defensively. The sharing Christian has little time for entertaining temptations. We are also in position to carry out a great raid on the enemy's POW camp. The gospel liberates captives — freeing them to begin the struggle themselves!

Proclaiming the gospel is not reserved for religious experts. Sharing the gospel of peace is part of "our struggle." A church or Christian without an evangelistic outreach is shoeless. How far can we get without shoes in rugged terrain? An army without equipment is lost, and this equipment is a cause, the message of peace. The *whole church* must carry the *whole gospel* to the *whole world*.

Clement of Alexandria describes the false teachers of his day as weak old shoes. The only thing that still works is the tongue. But with God's shoes we will do more than talk. We'll "go into all the world and preach the gospel . . ." (Mark 16:15).

The Bodyshield of Faith (6:16)

"In every situation taking up the shield of faith, by which you will be able to quench all the flaming arrows of the evil one."[1] In our struggle with evil we must expect a counterattack. The famous "Battle of the Bulge" in World War II caught the allied forces napping. They thought the enemy was too weak to fight back. It is foolish to think that our resourceful enemy will let us get away without subtle counterattacks or more open assaults. Faith is the shield that counters these blows. Shield as used by Paul here is not the Roman soldier's short shield, but his great, long bodyshield. It means protection from tip to toe by reliance on God.

Faith is trust in the competence of God. We can depend on God. "God is loyal . . ." (1 Cor. 1:9).[1] Naive Christians may believe that just because they are now on the winning side the struggle is over. Not so! Even though victory is assured, the struggle still goes on. We have changed sides and are now in a position to use God's armor, but we need faith to assure victory. "This is the victory that overcomes the world, our faith . . ." (1 John 5:4).

When Satan slings his flaming arrows our way we may be tempted to think God does not care. We should remember that Satan would not assault a conquered fortress.

The victory is ours, but we must not lose heart. Faith can put us in touch with God's power and strength. One dispirited believer found himself feeling defeated and discouraged by the activities of the evil one. He quickly recognized the defeatist symptoms in his heart which tempted him to sign an armistice with the devil. He wrote these lines to remind us to hold onto our shield.

Is there something in me
Like a beaten army,
Fleeing from a victory already won?

The Helmet of Salvation (6:17a) confidence

"Take the helmet of salvation . . . . " Putting on the

172

helmet meant only one thing to the Roman soldier, the battle was on. A soldier carried his helmet until he saw the enemy, then he put it on.

Salvation introduces us to the battle. When we are on the road to salvation we have confidence in the ultimate victory and protection for our mental outlook. The Lord's people are supposed to have enough confidence in the Lord and realize He wants them to be saved. God planned Christ's death and resurrection to create confident people. When we fail to have confidence in our salvation, we fail to have confidence in the cross. A soldier in battle without a helmet would soon regret his carelessness. A Christian without a concept of God's assuring power will not survive the battle.

Salvation means rescue or deliverance. It is a strong word. Something was done for us because we were in no condition to do anything for ourselves. A life preserver thrown out to a drowning man must be grasped, and we must put on the helmet of salvation. Accepting it means confidence in the God who has fashioned our salvation. As long as we depend on Jesus, we have assurance.

Jesus did not come to create a rag-tag, dispirited army with no confidence in their leader. When you put this helmet on, you have real protection.

The Spirit's Sword (6:17b)

"Take . . . the sword of the Spirit, which is the word of God...." Here is a powerful weapon to be used for both offense and defense. It is not our sword, it is the Spirit's. We did not forge this sword, design it, or sharpen it. But we must use it. That's why it is given to us. The Spirit convicts the world of sin, righteousness, and coming judgment when we use his sword (John 16:8).

A Roman soldier had to spend many hours to become familiar with his sword. When I served in the U.S. Marine Corps, our weapons were frequently inspected. Woe to that man with a rusty rifle! Woe to that man who could not handle his weapon! We spent blistering days on the rifle range firing our weapons. Hours were spent in the classroom learning how to take care of the weapon. No one expected to snap off some spontaneous shot from the hip like a cinema cowboy. Many hours of hard work, were needed to qualify as an expert rifleman.

You do not graduate from Bible study after a short course. Even a lifetime of study will hardly suffice. Knowing a few parts of a weapon is no substitute for actually using it in battle. For the word to become truly effective we must apply it in real-life situations. Jesus did just that in his temptation in the wilderness (Matt. 4:1-11). Jesus refused to let the sword of the Spirit go. He refused to be separated from his spiritual resources.

A soldier must not expect his fellow warriors to do his sword work for him. We need to depend on our brothers and sisters in the Lord for help, but not as spiritual parasites. We must use our sword ourselves. Some of us have lived off the fat of other people's studies too long. We cannot coast on other people's power. Paul expects every believer to pick up his sword and do his part in the struggle. We must put out individual effort, then each soldier side by side, will make an invincible wall in the Lord!

Battlefield Communication (6:18-22)

Many discussions of the Christian armor end with the sword of the Spirit (6:17). But Paul doesn't end there. In fact, he doesn't even break the sentence off, but continues it right on into verse 20! The point is obvious. You can outfit a soldier with the best of weapons and send him out into the struggle well-prepared. But if he fails to maintain communication with headquarters, he will soon find himself in trouble. He will find himself running low on supplies or needing direction from one who can see things in far greater perspective than he can. He will need to have constant communication to be a truly effective fighter for the Lord.

The Lord has not asked us to battle alone. He maintained constant communication with the Father while on earth (Mark 1:35). How successful could he have been without this communication? No wonder the army of the Lord becomes so disorganized and morale drops so low. Communication is not going on with Headquarters!

Paul advises us to "pray at every opportunity in the Spirit through total prayer and petition and in accomplishing this very result to continue alertly with all endurance and petition concerning all those who are dedicated, and on my behalf also . . ." (6:18, 19a).[1] Prayer is not optional, it is essential.

Another dimension emerges in Paul's discussion of prayer: alertness to opportunity and prayer. A sleeping sentry can endanger his whole outfit in wartime. A group of defeatist, sleepy-headed believers will overlook every good opportunity.

They will be, like the one-talent man, "afraid" to venture out for the Lord.

America's decisive losses at Pearl Harbor at the start of World War II could have been avoided by more alertness. Adequate warning was given by a radar outpost in Hawaii, but an officer told the radarmen it was just a flight of our own planes coming in from the States. Instead it was the Japanese attack force! An alert Christian is not going to be taken by surprise. Alertness to the situation on earth and communication with the Father in heaven are twin keys to victory in our struggle. "Watch and pray . . ." (Matt. 26:41).

A Final Word

Looking forward to sharing the undying love of Jesus with all God's soldiers is reason enough to carry on the struggle. We can now see the great purpose of Paul's letter. We have been impressed with the magnificent grace of God and have responded to this grace in faith. We sadly remember the wasted years apart from Jesus. But now in Jesus, we renounce all our old ways and allow ourselves to be clothed in the new man. We also have seen that this new, spiritually-motivated man accepts the guidance of God in all relationships. Throughout each phase of spiritual growth he realizes the Lord's power is continually sustaining him as he shares in the great victory. The Christian is now absolutely certain of being "chosen for riches."

The Whole church must carry Whole gospel to Whole world.